60
*Seconds
to Mind
Expansion*

60
Seconds
to Mind
Expansion

~~~~~~~~~~~~

Harold Cook
& Joel Davitz

Random House (New York

Library of Congress Cataloging in Publication Data
Cook, Harold.
60 seconds to mind expansion.
1. Consciousness. I. Davitz, Joel Robert,
joint author. II. Title.
BF311.C67   158   75–10294
ISBN 0–394–49797–X

Manufactured in the United States of America
2 3 4 5 6 7 8 9
First Edition

To aid the mind's development, to watch
Thy dawn of little joys, to sit and see
Almost thy very growth, to view thee catch
Knowledge of objects,—wonders yet to thee!

—CXVI *Childe Harold's Pilgrimage*
Lord Byron

Contents

60
Seconds
to Mind
Expansion

Introduction

What do you do with the moments in between? The 60 seconds, the minutes, and occasionally the hours, of waiting and nothingness. Those pieces of time spent waiting for a train, a bus, or standing in a cashier's line—the restless moments that all of us have before the waiter brings the menu or while the gas tank is being filled.

For most of us, such moments are experienced as boredom, and when we are not unspeakably bored during these waiting times, we are simply irritated by them. But neither the boredom nor the irritation is inevitable, for it is precisely these moments that can be most useful to us. Instead of being helplessly idle in these in-between times, we can be stimulated, creative, and relaxed. Instead of viewing such moments as "trapped" time, they can be seen as "free" time—time in which we are free to develop our senses, expand our consciousness, and exchange nothingness for awareness.

Most people would like to develop keener sensory response and expand their range of conscious awareness, but they think they don't have the time. Once they realize that waiting time is really available time, that obstacle disappears. Other people are hesitant to explore their inner lives and perceptions because they believe it requires embracing some ideological or philosophical doctrine. Quite the contrary is true. Long periods of special training are not necessary, nor is involvement with an ideology or philosophy a requirement. Without drugs, without dogma, without magic or mysticism, we can discover and get in touch with a world of experience that will enrich our lives. The purpose of this book is to make that world accessible.

We begin by describing some basic principles of consciousness and awareness. Then, a series of exercises based on these principles is presented. The first exercises are relatively short and simple, becoming longer and somewhat more complex as the technique is mastered.

Read each exercise through twice. Then try it, keeping in mind that the exercises are not solutions to all the multifaceted problems of living. They will not result in instant Zen, overnight Yoga, or immediate Nirvana. They involve the reader in the application of some psychological principles necessary to fulfilling a fundamental human need— the expansion of the mind. Moreover, these exercises offer freedom from the concept of "wasted" time. They will help you to see more, feel more, experience more. Finally, they provide invaluable opportunities for unwinding, relaxing and eliminating tension. Learning to live intensely while learning to live gently—that is what this book is all about.

Basic
Principles

~~~~~~~~~~~~~~~~~

1) *How to Focus*

As you read these words, there are dozens of things—objects, sensations, and feelings—that you are *not* aware of. Have you noticed the color of this paper? Its texture? The shape of the book? Are you aware of the sounds in the room? Are there sounds coming from outside? If you are standing up, are you conscious of the pressure on the bottom of your feet? If you are sitting down, are you aware of the pressure on your backside? Are you feeling irritable, joyous, or peaceful?

We could go on like this for some time, listing the stimuli that are probably impinging upon you from both internal and external sources. But suffice it to say that until this moment, you were probably unaware of the great majority of them. As a matter of fact, you couldn't be reading and understanding these words, and at the same time be conscious of all the stimuli bombarding you.

For the most part the world of potential stimuli exists for us at a subliminal level, below the threshold of consciousness. Our awareness is like the beam of a focused flashlight.

We can see the spot it shines on, and perhaps a bit around the edges, but the rest is darkness and unawareness until we shift the light.

There is nothing mysterious about this. It is simply a natural consequence of the human nervous system. Each of us needs and can tolerate only so much stimulation; each of us functions within a more or less narrow band of awareness. If there is too little stimulation over a period of time, we become stimulus-hungry, and we begin searching out stimuli in the external world or generating our own internal stimulation in daydreams and fantasy. If there is too much going on, our normal functioning is disrupted and we are likely to become tense, irritable, and uncomfortable. Imagine trying to read these words while in the middle of a boiler factory. With too much stimulation, the system is overloaded and reading becomes impossible. In a sense, we live in the middle of a potential boiler factory. In our normal, everyday world there are almost always too many stimuli to be perceived. Therefore, we must focus awareness, limit consciousness and restrict our attention. We could not function otherwise and life would be unbearable. Consciousness and attention must be *selective* and *discriminating*.

2) *Creating Consciousness*

Human beings are not passive recorders of the world's events. Rather, we actively participate in the interactions between events and ourselves—all of which determine our awareness. Suppose that, for one reason or another, you have not had a chance to eat all day, and as you are coming home from work, you feel the pangs of hunger. As you walk down the street, chances are that you will be particularly sensitive to cues or clues related to food. Perhaps you will notice a grocery store that you never noticed before; maybe you will pay special attention to some food displayed in a shop window; you might even notice and deeply inhale that sudden smell of bread baking as you walk past a bakery on the block. You may have walked this way many times before and never been aware of how many food-related cues there were. But this time, there is a difference: you are hungry. You might even become aware of an increase in the flow of your saliva. The consciousness you create is influenced by that hunger.

Similarly, the person who becomes interested in tennis suddenly notices how many articles and advertisements in the newspaper are related to tennis—sales of tennis rackets, tennis clothing, tennis clubs, etc. If you have decided to buy a new car, you become conscious of the many different kinds of cars there are on the streets these days. If you are getting a cold, have a headache, a sore throat, your bones ache, you experience the world as depressing, a dull and dingy place. If your loved one or friend develops arthritis or pulls a tendon, very likely your own body starts aching.

In each instance, internal processes influence and focus your awareness. Your drives, interests, goals, your physical as well as your psychological state make a difference in the consciousness you experience.

External events, of course, also make a difference. If a growling lion were to walk into the room you are in, your state of consciousness surely would be altered, as it would if you were suddenly called upon to give a talk on trout fishing to a roomful of people. But it is not just the physical event of the growling lion or the roomful of people that causes the effect; it is the way *you* see, interpret and experience the physical event. Consciousness is a consequence of the interaction between the event and the experiencing human being. We are not automatic focusing cameras or mechanical tape recorders that simply respond when stimulated; we actively and humanly create our own awareness and consciousness.

3) *Getting Set to Perceive*

As you read this sentence, your eye does not stop to look at every single letter on the page. You don't have to. You can read the page rapidly, using far fewer cues than the print actually contains. This is possible because you are *set* to perceive printed English. On the basis of past experience, certain expectancies have been built up, and without looking at every letter, you can "see" the words while scanning the page. This ability to scan can be facilitated by practice. Just look at the effect of speed-reading courses—they teach you to aggressively and actively scan the page.

All of us develop certain perceptual sets that help to focus our attention. As indicated earlier, no one can perceive everything that is potentially available to the senses. Perception and consciousness must be selective, and one important basis for selectivity in any situation is our set to perceive. Other things being equal, we tend to see what we expect to see, because that is what we look for, what we focus on. When we visit a dentist's office, we expect to see popular-type, out-of-date magazines, hear Muzak, and observe quietly anxious patients in the waiting room. We may very well fail to notice the original Rembrandt drawing on the wall, because that is not what we are set to see in a dentist's office. When we go to a concert, we expect to see musicians and hear the music they play. We probably don't notice the color of the carpet in the hall or the face of the man who takes the tickets. When we look at our watch, we attend to the time and are barely aware of the big and little hand positions. We generally don't notice the kind of numerals or other decorative features. In fact, if you try to draw the face of your watch, you'll see how difficult it is to make an accurate replica, though you have looked at it a hundred, or perhaps a thousand, times. It is not that we are particularly insensitive, but that carpets, ticket takers, and shapes of numerals are not part of the *perceptual set* generally thought of in association with concerts or watches.

In view of the fact that our state of consciousness depends, in part, on what we perceive, consciousness is clearly influenced by our perceptual sets. Notice, for example, that there is a certain repetitive quality about your day-to-day consciousness. Part of this is due to the fact that everyone tends to be in more or less the same situations from day to day. We often react automatically, but the repetitive quality is emphasized by the perceptual set to attend to very much the same cues in situations we encounter repeatedly. If we take a bus to work every weekday morning, we pretty much notice the same things each day. We say good morning to people; expect to hear good morning back, and that is probably what we do "hear," regardless of what other people might be saying. Of course, we don't live completely within our perceptual sets. If the bus came along being pulled by six reindeer, we'd probably notice that. And if someone greeted our good morning with the news that he had just won the Irish Sweepstakes, we'd probably hear it regardless of perceptual sets. In other words, there are limits to the influence of perceptual sets, but there are also limits to the variability of events we are likely to meet. Reindeer pulling buses and winning Irish Sweepstakes are not everyday events. The majority of us live in much more predictable worlds.

Just as perceptual sets regarding language make reading more efficient, so too do other sets make other aspects of life much easier. As a result of our daily experiences, we learn what to look for, what to listen for, what to expect. We don't always have to be functioning at top capacity, constantly scanning and evaluating our environment. We can idle along at a more comfortable pace, relying on the efficiency of our perceptual skills and accumulated habits.

At the same time, though, our consciousness is bound to be limited by the sets we develop. This is the price we pay for efficiency, and sometimes the price may be very high. We cannot live without selectively perceiving, and a large part of this selectivity depends upon our sets to perceive. This makes life easier, more efficient, and frequently more effective; but it also narrows our range of consciousness and limits our awareness of the subtleties of potentially enriching experiences.

4) How Thinking Affects Consciousness

Even brief contact with another culture through travel, a book, a movie, or from television reveals that our own way of thinking is not the only way. It is merely one of many possibilities—and not always the best, most useful, or most valid way of thought.

Moreover, differences in the way we think make a difference in the way we experience the world. For example, when someone we know becomes ill, we think about the illness in terms of various disease processes—bacteria, viruses, infection; and we usually think of treatment in terms of medication—drugs, surgery, or some other form of medical therapy. We "experience" the illness, explain it, understand it, and are conscious of it as a natural phenomenon, as part of our physical world that can be rationally and objectively understood. In another culture, the same symptoms, the same objective events might be experienced in an altogether different way. Rather than a natural phenomenon, it might be thought of as a manifestation of a supernatural force, or a spirit, perhaps understood as the consequences of an evil spell, to be treated by exorcism, counter-spells, or prayer. It is not only a matter of different words and a different explanation, but a different conscious experience. Thinking about an event in different ways makes the experience of that event also different.

We need not go to other cultures for illustration. For that matter, we need not even compare one person with another in the same culture. Consider your own experiences before and after learning how to deal with some complex problems. It might be a problem in mathematics; it might involve some technical phenomenon, such as learning how to put together a stereophonic amplifier, or how to figure the annual interest your bank pays; it might even be the understanding of some complex, personal, psychological problem or a complicated social issue. At first, your experience might be largely confusion, discomfort, frustration. Nothing seems to make sense. It appears mysterious, disorganized, jumbled. But then you learn how to think about it, and as your thinking changes, so too does your conscious experience. Confusion is replaced by order, frustration by satisfaction, and the mysterious becomes rational, often obvious and easy. You might even wonder how you could have ever thought it was so confusing. Your way of thinking about the phenomenon changed your way of experiencing it.

Because thinking influences consciousness, and our goal is to help you understand how to expand consciousness, it is obviously important to clarify what we mean by thinking. It can be described as ways of representing the world to oneself in symbols. And the most important one is language. To a certain extent, then, consciousness is determined by the language one uses to think. Language not only coordinates our thinking, and therefore our conscious experience, but it is also our chief means of communicating with one another. Consider what we as authors are doing right now. We wish to communicate with you, and we are doing it with words. Although communication can take place in nonverbal ways, and these are unquestionably important, words remain our primary means of communication.

In order to communicate, both parties have to use symbols in pretty much the same way. If we used our language in one way, and you used it in another, obviously we would not understand each other. Therefore, all of us within a given language community have to learn and agree to use conventional language symbols. There are dictionary meanings of words, and there are grammatical rules that govern how words go together. In addition, there are certain ideas, general concepts or connotations of words that all of us in the same culture have learned and accepted. Our understanding of "disease" was used to illustrate a commonly shared concept. There are many, many more shared concepts that make communication possible.

The same symbolic system used to communicate with others is used to think. Our thinking, therefore, is necessarily influenced by the conventions of that system, for it reflects and is structured by them. The ways we experience the world also reflect those conventions. When we learn to speak so that we make sense to others, we are also learning to focus, limit, and narrow our conscious experience. To expand our consciousness, we have to learn how to break or change some of these conventions, at least temporarily, to allow ourselves to experience the world in new ways.

If you cross the street after reading this today, we hope you won't be thinking about mind expansion. You had better be watching for cars and trucks, and maybe for open manholes. If you go to work today, we hope you don't spend too much time thinking about mind expansion. If you do, probably little work will get done.

We live in a world of pragmatic demands. There are streets to be crossed, jobs to be done, responsibilities to fulfill. For almost all of us, reality consists largely of the everyday problems of living, and our perceptions, our thinking, our consciousness, must be geared to this plane of reality. But the pragmatic is *not the only* plane of reality. Even the most practical among us can live, at times, free from the demands of everyday life. There is nothing wrong with the pragmatic, the practical per se; the only danger comes when the pragmatic view dictates all of our conscious experience. If we cannot look at a street without thinking of the dangers of crossing, our consciousness is obviously limited and blocked. If we awaken in the morning and can think only of the jobs to be done that day, we are living only partial lives. If the pragmatic determines *all* of our consciousness, we are committing psychological suicide.

5) *Creating New Ways to Think*

We can expand our consciousness by breaking old habits of thinking and by creating new ones. This proposition is the basis of our work. All of the exercises that follow are based on that assumption. Each exercise is designed to counteract old habits of perceiving and thinking, and to foster new ones.

A word of caution before you begin. In any new pursuit, there is sometimes a tendency to rush through the initial steps and expect expertise today—or at the latest, tomorrow. Don't! Don't rush, and don't expect miracles overnight. Rushing will ruin the process; it is the antithesis of living gently and experiencing widely. It is likely that this rush for awareness is an old set which may have even prompted you to read this book. Take it easily, comfortably, leisurely—but also take it seriously and consistently. If you rush through the exercises today and then drop them for a week or a month, nothing much will happen. The gymnast can't just quickly do a few exercises and then hope he remains in shape without continual exercise. Your consciousness won't evaporate; your potential won't disappear. But don't expect any dramatic change.

We are reluctant to suggest anything like a schedule. It sounds too much like school or a job. But as a general guide, we suggest you begin with some of the shorter warm-up exercises. Read an exercise through twice so that you're familiar with it. You then will have some idea of what to expect. Try them all a few times until you feel you are getting the hang of it. Select one, perhaps two or three, that seem to fit you best, and use them repeatedly for a time.

Try beginning with the 6o-second exercises. We suggest you keep a brief diary of your experiences so that you can keep track of how your consciousness develops and changes. Don't bother about a regular time each day; if you miss a day or two, don't worry about it. Stay loose, stay easy. Exercise when you have a moment free; an in-between moment on the way to work, a minute during a break, while waiting for lunch, while bathing, standing in line, on the bus, in bed, at the supermarket. Whenever 6o seconds of nothingness occurs.

Gradually work your way into the longer exercises. Don't push it; do what comes naturally. Find the exercises that work for you, and stick with them. Use them as a model, but feel comfortable to develop your own variations, your own style. You can develop your own ways of mind expansion, for if this book is successful, it will become unnecessary, like the elementary-school reader that you have long forgotten.

But a miracle? No! This is not the way of miracles. No sudden, magically overwhelming insights will come gushing forth; no violent ecstasy, no emotional orgasms will sweep you away. Instead, if you pursue the exercises steadily, consistently, your consciousness will expand in slow and easy stages, often without awareness of your own growth. You will find it interesting to go back and look at your notes of your experiences and the subtle changes you may have recorded—as you would look back with a smile at a photograph from childhood. Some moment in the future, at a time of reflection, you will recognize that your moments of nothingness are fewer and far between; your mind has discovered new dimensions of awareness, and you are living gently.

60-Second Warm-ups

~~~~~~~~~~~~~

This first set of exercises is designed to sharpen your sensory awareness. We look, listen, taste, and touch, but in the pace of everyday life, our senses become dulled and diluted. To refresh your senses, take a 60-second break—not to look but to *see*, not to hear but to *listen*, to *relish* rather than taste, to *really feel* rather than merely touch.

Seeing

Find a quiet place where you will be uninterrupted for at least 60 seconds. You may be at home or at work, perhaps in a restaurant waiting to be served or in a station waiting for the bus. Anywhere—the place doesn't matter as long as you have 60 seconds free from outside intrusions. Don't worry about whether it's *exactly* 60 seconds. You will develop a feel for various time segments. Now sit down, relax, and harness your energies for 60 seconds of intense concentration.

PICK UP A SMALL OBJECT,

A PENCIL, A COIN, A KEY.

ANYTHING THAT'S HANDY, THAT YOU HAVE LOOKED AT A THOUSAND TIMES BUT NEVER REALLY SEEN BEFORE.

NOW HOLD IT IN FRONT OF YOU.

FOCUS ON IT AND LOOK!

DON'T THINK ABOUT IT;

DON'T ANALYZE IT;

DON'T TALK ABOUT IT.

JUST EXPERIENCE IT DIRECTLY, WORDLESSLY, VISUALLY.

CONCENTRATE ON THE OBJECT AS YOU LOOK AT IT.

NOTICE THE OVERALL SHAPE,

THE COLORS, THE IMPERFECTIONS, THE BUMPS, THE SCRATCHES,

THE LITTLE THINGS THAT MAKE THIS COIN, THIS PENCIL, UNIQUE.

THE WAYS IN WHICH THIS OBJECT IS DIFFERENT FROM EVERYTHING ELSE IN THE WORLD.

Hold it. Sixty seconds of intense, focused concentration is enough for a start. Without thinking about the experience, go back to what you were doing; try not to think about the experience; let your mind wander back to where it was. Sometime later, find another 60-second break.

RELAX,

AND THEN CONCENTRATE AS BEFORE.

CONCENTRATE ON REALLY LOOKING AT AN OBJECT.

FOCUSED CONCENTRATION—THAT IS THE SECRET.

ALL OF YOUR ENERGIES,

ALL OF YOUR ATTENTION

FOCUSED ON LOOKING

AND THEN SEEING.

FOR THOSE 6o SECONDS FREE YOUR MIND.

SOUNDS ARE NOTHING;

THOUGHTS ARE NOTHING;

THE REST OF THE WORLD IS NOTHING.

THERE IS ONLY THE OBJECT OF YOUR LOOKING

AND THE EXPERIENCE OF YOUR SEEING.

You have gone through the basic exercise twice. Don't expect any immediate miracles; your world isn't going to change in a moment just because you've looked once, or looked twice—and maybe *seen* just a bit. This is merely the beginning—but it is a beginning. You are training yourself to focus, to concentrate, to exclude all the rest of the world and to open yourself up entirely to seeing. It is not easy, nor is it that difficult; this seemingly simplest of acts contains the core of the beginnings of experiencing an expanded consciousness, and while the aim is utter simplicity, you must exercise and practice to achieve it.

At first, there may be questions. What do I look for? How do I know I am seeing? Just look, concentrate on looking at small parts and aspects of objects—and you'll see. As you practice, you will discover that 60 seconds is far too short a time to see everything there is to be seen. Stop questioning; your looking will provide the answers. You'll see things you've never seen before in 60 seconds and, hopefully, your awareness will spread across your environment.

Other objects will cross your visual field; sounds will be heard; the rest of the world will be battering the walls of your concentration trying to get in. STAY FOCUSED; STAY WITHIN YOURSELF; gradually, slowly, the rest of the world will appear to disappear, and you can look— and you *will* see. But guard against your own thoughts, your own words, your internal world that gets in the way of direct experience. We are word animals, analyzing, thinking animals—but for now, for 60 seconds, drop the words, drop the thinking, experience directly, fully, visually.

Exercise again, and again—and again, whenever you have a moment. Only 60 seconds at a time; in the beginning, we can achieve fullest concentration only for very brief periods. But practice—once a day, twice, three times, whenever there is a moment of static existence. Then gradually, you will see shapes and curves you have never seen before; you will see colors and shadows, lines and textures, differences and distinctions of a new world discovered in the most common objects of your everyday life. It is all there, waiting to be seen, but you must acquire the capacity for seeing, for focused, concentrated vision. And after a while, the simplicity will come. What once was simple will be simple again, but with a difference. For you will look, and you will see—and you will know the difference.

Listening

We live in a world of sounds—the chatter of voices, the honking of horns, the subtle, pervasive everyday noises of paper rustling, footsteps, creaking floors, doors and fans, cars and wind. To live in this babel of noises, we have learned *not* to hear, we have learned to close off the channel of constant never-ending noise. But now, we're ready to re-learn; to re-experience.

We pay the price of psychological deafness, and we are hard of hearing because it *is* hard to listen—and to hear. But with practice, we can learn. You are on a busy street corner, at a crowded party where many different conversations are occurring, on the beach, in the woods, in the relative quiet of your own living room, or at the supermarket. Now, listen.

FOR 6o SECONDS, STOP, DON'T MOVE.

ARMS HANG LIMPLY AT YOUR SIDES;

FEET ARE STILL; ALL BODY MOTION STOPS.

LOWER YOUR CHIN; HEAD DOWN.

CLOSE YOUR EYES.

QUIET; ATTEND; FOCUS.

LISTEN WITH CARE.

AT FIRST A JUMBLE OF SOUND?

LISTEN WITH CARE.

STOP THINKING; STOP FIGURING OUT; STOP NAMING THE SOUNDS,

JUST LISTEN AND EXPERIENCE THIS WORLD OF SOUNDS.

SIXTY SECONDS ARE UP.

STOP; RETURN TO YOUR EVERYDAY WORLD.

RETURN TO WHAT YOU WERE DOING.

DON'T THINK ABOUT WHAT YOU HAVE HEARD.

GO ON LIVING AMONG THE SOUNDS OF YOUR WORLD.

BUT THEN,

WHENEVER YOU HAVE 60-SECONDS,

STOP, ATTEND.

BUILD YOUR CONCENTRATION;

FOCUS; FORGET YOURSELF; EXIST ONLY IN SOUND.

ONE SOUND STANDS OUT—

THE FIGURE AGAINST THE GROUND.

LISTEN.

HEAR THE PITCH? FOLLOW IT. STAY WITH IT.

SENSE THE RHYTHM AND THE CHANGE;

DOES IT FADE INTO THE BACKGROUND?

DOES IT GROW—OR STAY THE SAME?

LISTEN.

PRACTICE; FOCUS; CONCENTRATE,

AGAIN—AND AGAIN—AND AGAIN.

DON'T THINK ABOUT IT,

DON'T LET WORDS GET IN THE WAY.

JUST LISTEN,

AND HEAR.

And then, one moment will be noise—and the next you *will* hear the wind and rain. You will hear melodies of everyday life—the songs, sometimes the symphonies. The ebbs and flows of sound. You will hear the concerto of a clock ticking against the orchestra of sounds in the room. You will hear rhythms and timbres, cymbals and bells, the plucked guitar—the music of a new world far richer in sounds than you have ever heard before.

Don't rush it. Go slow. Pace yourself. Practice easily, comfortably, consistently. But not too much. Gradually open yourself to this world, without pushing, without strain. Not too much at one time. Practice 60 seconds at a time, whenever you have a moment—and eventually even you will hear the quiet sound of silence.

Relishing

For this exercise, we suggest you wait until you're just a bit hungry. Not starving, but when you feel like you're ready to eat—wanting to taste. You could do it before breakfast, lunch, dinner—or before that midnight snack. Take small pieces of bread, crackers, or some other kind of food that isn't too sweet or spicy—something in the middle range, something you like. Put the food on a plate. Sit down at a table with the food in front of you. Look directly at the food without shifting your glance. Put it in your mouth.

FOCUS ON YOUR MOUTH, YOUR TONGUE, YOUR LIPS.

FEEL YOUR TEETH WITH YOUR TONGUE,

SLOWLY—SLOWLY—CHEW.

EASY; TASTE; CHEW; SLOWLY; SWALLOW; TASTE—

STOP.

DON'T THINK. JUST FEEL; TASTE; RELISH.

Again; another 60 seconds . . .

CONCENTRATE ON YOUR TONGUE, ON THE INSIDE OF YOUR MOUTH.

PUT A SMALL PIECE OF FOOD ON YOUR TONGUE.

HOLD IT ON YOUR TONGUE;

FEEL IT, ROLL IT

UP AGAINST THE TOP OF YOUR MOUTH,

GENTLY; TO ONE SIDE; THE OTHER;

BACK AND FORTH, AND

RELISH THE TASTE.

SLOWLY CHEW,

GENTLY SWALLOW,

TASTE THE FOOD.

AGAIN, CHEW, TASTE THE FOOD. SWALLOW.

STOP. GO BACK TO WHAT YOU WERE DOING.

When you feel a bit hungry again . . .

STOP; FOCUS; ATTEND.

TAKE A BITE, A SMALL BIT OF FOOD.

TASTE IT.

MOVE IT AROUND IN YOUR MOUTH WITH THE TIP OF YOUR TONGUE.

FEEL THE SHAPE, THE TEXTURE, AND

CONCENTRATE.

FEEL THE WEIGHT OF THE FOOD, AND WITH YOUR TONGUE

PUSH IT AGAINST YOUR TEETH.

GENTLY, SLOWLY, CHEW AND TASTE.

SLOWLY, SWALLOW, TASTE AND RELISH,

STOP.

Again . . .

PUT A BIT OF FOOD IN YOUR MOUTH.

FEEL IT; ROLL IT AGAINST THE ROOF OF YOUR MOUTH.

CHEW; TASTE; GENTLY RUB YOUR TOP TEETH AGAINST YOUR BOTTOM TEETH;

CHEW AND TASTE. SLOWLY. CHEW.

NOW EXPERIENCE THE TASTE.

Again, put the food in your mouth . . .

ROLL IT AROUND.

PUSH THE FOOD AGAINST YOUR CHEEK.

AROUND. NOW FEEL IT. ATTEND TO THE FEELING.

CHEW AND THEN SWALLOW A TINY BIT.

TASTE IT.

SLOWLY PUSH THE FOOD AGAINST THE BACK OF YOUR FRONT TEETH.

SLOWLY; CONCENTRATE; MOVE THE FOOD WITH YOUR TONGUE.

CHEW, AND THEN SLOWLY TASTE AND SWALLOW.

STOP.

DON'T THINK ABOUT IT.

LET LITTLE BITS AND PIECES OF FOOD AWAKEN
YOUR AWARENESS OF TASTE.

SENSE THE EXPERIENCE FULLY, AND RELISH IT.

~~~~~~~~~~~

Feeling

Now you have some sense of how the exercises go. As we said earlier, there is nothing magical or mystical about the exercises; they simply get you in touch with your senses—directly, immediately, without the filters and blinders we build and use in our everyday lives. At first the exercises may appear simple, but as you practice and experience them, you will move deeper into sensory awareness, and you'll begin to appreciate their difficulty, subtlety, and complexity. Impressions get muddled; thoughts interfere; words come and get in the way. You might capture a glimpse, have a brief glimmer, and then it fades. You might feel as if you are rich one day, and poor the next. You do not grow in a single, straight line. You are up, then down; open, then closed. The process is slow, and awareness develops gradually.

In short, you are human, and your consciousness grows as human consciousness always grows, in jagged leaps and falls, successes and frustrations. You move toward and then away from awareness, but gradually, inevitably, deepening and expanding your consciousness.

Continue to practice seeing, listening and relishing. In a very real sense, you are exercising your "sensory muscles," and the more consistently you exercise, the sharper and more sensitive your senses will become. So in the 60 seconds in between—in the moments of your freedom—stop, look, and listen; and you will be seeing, listening and relishing.

Now, let's concentrate on the experience of direct and intense touch. Pick up any small, common object. It might be the same one you've used in your seeing exercise, or it might be something entirely different. A piece of cloth, a piece of wood, a rubber ball, a paper clip. You might start with a stone, a pebble, or a sea shell that you picked up somewhere. Hold it in your hands. Don't look at it. Save it for feeling; discover it only through touch.

FOCUS, AND NOW CONCENTRATE.

LIGHTLY, GENTLY, TAP IT WITH THE TIPS OF YOUR FINGERS.

ROLL IT IN YOUR PALM.

HOLD IT. FEEL ITS WEIGHT.

DON'T THINK ABOUT IT; NO WORDS; JUST FOCUS AND ATTEND TO YOUR SENSE OF TOUCH.

SLOWLY SHIFT IT IN YOUR HANDS.

FEEL THE PRESSURE AGAINST YOUR FINGERS, AGAINST YOUR PALMS. FEEL THE WEIGHT SHIFT AS IT MOVES THROUGH YOUR HANDS.

LET IT LIE IN ONE HAND.

REST. STOP.

GO BACK TO WHAT YOU WERE DOING.

DON'T THINK ABOUT THE EXERCISE.

Another break; another 60 seconds . . .

PICK UP A STONE.

DON'T LOOK AT THE STONE.

RUB YOUR FINGERS OVER IT.

LET ALL THE EXPERIENCE FLOW THROUGH YOUR FINGERS;
BECOME AWARE OF THE FEELING.

DISCOVER ITS SHAPE.

WITH CARE, AND SLOWLY, GENTLY FEEL THE CONTOURS.

FEEL THE SMOOTHNESS, THE ROUGHNESS, THE LINES,
THE BREAKS;

CONCENTRATE AND FOCUS;

FEEL THE TINY BUMPS, THE TEXTURE.

RUB IT WITH YOUR FINGERS, BACK AND FORTH,
BACK AND FORTH.

STOP; 60 SECONDS ARE UP.

GO BACK TO WHAT YOU WERE DOING.

Again, another 60 seconds free . . .

PICK UP THE STONE.

RUB IT BACK AND FORTH; SLOWLY, GENTLY.

ATTEND TO HOW IT FEELS IN YOUR FINGERS, IN YOUR
HANDS.

NOW CHANGE DIRECTIONS; RUB IT EASILY, GENTLY;

RUB IT HARDER. HARDER.

NOW EVEN HARDER.

SLOW DOWN. GENTLY AGAIN.

FEEL INTO THE STONE; EXPERIENCE THE FEELING.

STOP.

Now put the stone to your face . . .

GENTLY TOUCH YOUR CHEEK.

NO WORDS; BUT FEEL IT; SENSE IT DIRECTLY.

INTENSELY THROUGH YOUR TOUCH WITHOUT WORDS WITHOUT THOUGHTS.

FOCUSED CONCENTRATION ON THE FEELINGS OF TOUCH; ROLL THE STONE ON YOUR CHEEK;

ACROSS YOUR FOREHEAD;

SLOWLY. BACK AGAINST YOUR CHEEK.

WARM? COLD? SMOOTH? ROUGH?

FOCUS ON TOUCHING AND FEELING.

STOP. PUT THE STONE DOWN AND RETURN TO WHAT YOU WERE DOING.

At some other time when you have a moment . . .

PICK UP THE STONE;

AND AGAIN, HOLD IT IN YOUR HANDS.

RUB THE STONE ALONG THE INSIDE OF YOUR ARM,

SLOWLY, GENTLY; STOP A MOMENT.

CONCENTRATE.

LET IT REST ON YOUR ARM,

FEEL IT RESTING.

HOLD IT AGAINST YOUR ARM;

FEEL DOWN BELOW THE SURFACE,

SLOWLY, LET IT COME INTO YOUR FINGERS; DON'T REACH;
DON'T PUSH; LET IT COME; FLOWING, DRIFTING SLOWLY,
SENSING ITS WAY INTO YOUR AWARENESS.

STOP. NOW SQUEEZE THE STONE HARDER.

RELAX.

THEN SQUEEZE HARDER AGAIN; GRADUALLY INCREASE THE
PRESSURE AS HARD AS YOU CAN. TIGHT; CLENCH.

EASE OFF; TOUCH IT WITH THE TIPS OF YOUR FINGERS;

SENSE ITS SHAPE, AROUND THE EDGES;

RUB, FEEL ITS WEIGHT; RUB AGAIN; CHANGE DIRECTIONS.

STOP; 60 SECONDS ARE UP.

~~~~~~~~~~

A stone. A simple, ordinary, common stone. But you
touched it, and you have discovered how to feel it. Practice.
Exercise. And it will become simple again.

Breathing and Breathing Again

Got 60 seconds? Relax. Get comfortable.
Breathing is the source of life—through these breathing
exercises you can feel and experience this source again. So
concentrate on breathing for 60 seconds—and savor the
freshness of breathing.
The simplest of the breathing exercises involves the concentration of awareness on 1) slowly—slowly inhaling; 2)
then holding your breath, and finally; 3) exhaling slowly.
The inhaling and exhaling should be done very slowly—
very slowly and through your nostrils.
Find a comfortable spot—on the grass of a park, a lawn,

on the floor, on a chair or couch, sitting at the kitchen table. Take off your shoes. Loosen a collar button, a belt, a necktie. Stretch out your legs, let your arms drop to your sides. Relax.

FOR 60 SECONDS, RELAX.

BREATHE IN SLOWLY,

RELAX.

HOLD IT; HOLD YOUR BREATH.

NOW SLOWLY, SLOWLY, EXHALE.

TWO SECONDS TO INHALE;

HOLD YOUR BREATH FOR 4;

NOW SLOWLY EXHALE IN 8 SECONDS—NO MORE.

BUILD UP THE RHYTHM,

TWO, FOUR, EIGHT;

TWO IN; FOUR HOLD; EIGHT OUT.

REGULAR, RHYTHMIC BREATH.

Sixty seconds again . . .

RELAX, AND INHALE THROUGH THE NOSTRILS,

SLOWLY; CONCENTRATE.

HOLD IT; BREATH OUT THROUGH THE MOUTH, COMPLETELY,

COMPLETELY AND EVER SO GENTLY.

CONTINUE AGAIN, IN REGULAR RHYTHM,

WITH FOCUSED CONCENTRATION.

IN; OUT; SLOWLY, GENTLY; BREATHE, AND

FOCUS COMPLETELY.

SENSE THE AIR COMING IN THROUGH YOUR NOSE;

SENSE YOUR BODY HOLDING STILL;

SENSE THE AIR GOING OUT THROUGH YOUR MOUTH;

KEEP UP THE RHYTHM, THE SAME EACH TIME;

GROW FULLY AWARE, TOTALLY CONSCIOUS

OF THE RHYTHM OF BREATHING AGAIN.

~~~~~~~~~~

Breathing is one of the automatic life processes, so automatic that we are rarely conscious of it. Yet it is an extraordinarily complex phenomenon, requiring delicate coordination and timing.

Awareness requires control, and control produces awareness. As you focus on your breathing, you'll be regulating it while your awareness of your body is enhanced. You can change the pattern of your breathing, its depth, and its rhythm, gaining thereby greater awareness of self.

Feeling Inward

Up to this point, by performing these exercises, you've been sharpening your senses—becoming more aware of some simple sensations, of little things around you. At the same time, you've been building your powers of concentration, your ability to focus your senses and attention, and break the superficial sets of your everyday perceptual world. Practice what you've experienced.

Now let us turn our attention to inner perception. Begin to discover your own body. Find a comfortable chair. Not too soft. Don't sink in. Sit *on* the chair, not in it. Sit back, straight but not rigid. Relax. Don't slouch, but sit easy, alert within yourself.

FOCUS ON PRECISELY THE POINT

WHERE YOUR RIGHT ARM JOINS YOUR SHOULDER.

CONCENTRATE ALL ENERGY ON THIS POINT.

NOW SLOWLY MOVE THE JOINT FORWARD, JUST A BIT;
AN INCH, PERHAPS TWO.

HOLD IT THERE JUST FOR A MOMENT;

NOW MOVE IT BACK AGAIN; AN INCH, SLOWLY, AN INCH.

AGAIN MOVE IT FORWARD AND BACK,

SLOWLY AND RHYTHMICALLY MOVE.

FEEL THE MUSCLES, THE JOINT, THE BONE;

FORWARD AND BACKWARD AGAIN.

DON'T PUSH IT; EASY; RELAX.

MOVE AND FEEL THE MOVEMENT.

BE THERE AT THAT POINT IN YOUR WORLD.

Again, for 60 seconds . . .

BACK TO THAT POINT; NOW FOCUS;

MOVE THE SHOULDER AROUND IN A CIRCLE;

A SLOWLY REVOLVING SMALL CIRCLE.

UP AND FORWARD, SLOWLY; DOWN AND AROUND, IN A
STEADY AND REGULAR RHYTHM.

SENSE THE INTERNAL FEELING, THE MOVEMENT,

THEN STOP. THEN MOVE IT AGAIN IN A CIRCLE.

AROUND ONCE AGAIN, AND FOCUS

YOUR TOTAL ATTENTION; AND FEEL IT;

FEEL THE BONE MOVE AROUND IN YOUR BODY;

FEEL THE SLIGHT, SMALL PRESSURES—AND EASE.

NOW STOP. RELAX. DON'T MOVE.

BACK TO YOUR EVERYDAY WORLD.

Find another 60 seconds. Sit down. Be comfortable. Relax,
but be alert within yourself.

FOCUS THIS TIME ON THE POINT WHERE YOUR LEFT
ARM JOINS THE SHOULDER.

REPEAT, AS DONE FOR THE RIGHT.

FORWARD, THEN BACK; AGAIN.

SLOWLY AND RHYTHMICALLY MOVE, FORWARD AND
BACK AGAIN.

ALL ATTENTION UPON THAT POINT.

For 60 seconds again . . .

WHERE THE LEFT ARM JOINS THE SHOULDER,

FOCUS UPON THAT POINT.

MOVE IT UP—AND OVER—DOWN—AND AROUND;

ONCE AND TWICE; AGAIN.

SENSE THE BONE MOVING, THE MUSCLE PULL A BIT.

NOW PULL THE POINT IN TOWARD YOUR BODY;

THEN OUT AGAIN——OUT——AND THEN NORMAL.

FEEL THE STRETCH AND THE PULL;

FEEL IT MOVE IN AND THEN OUT; EASY, THEN BACK.

STOP. NOW GO BACK TO YOUR WORLD.

For 60 seconds, sit.

YOU ARE ALERT AND FOCUSED INWARD.

PULL YOUR FOCUS WITHIN, AND SENSE YOUR INNER
SELF.

CONCENTRATE FULLY ON THE PIT OF YOUR STOMACH;

FOCUS AND FIND THE POINT.

WASH YOUR THINKING AWAY, BLANK, AND TURN WITHIN;

FEEL DOWN THROUGH YOUR BODY, THROUGH THE CHEST
TO THE PIT,

THE SINGLE POINT CENTER OF YOU.

MOVE IT OUT JUST A FRACTION——

BACK IN AGAIN.

FEEL THE SMALLEST OF MOVEMENTS IN YOU.

AGAIN, OUT AND IN; FOCUS; AGAIN.

NOW MOVE IT AROUND IN A CIRCLE.

FEEL YOURSELF IN YOURSELF.

AROUND AGAIN;

STOP. COME BACK. MOVE ABOUT.

Come out of your static existence for 60 seconds again.

SIT UP STRAIGHT AND COMFORTABLY; FEET FLAT ON THE FLOOR.

FOCUS INWARD, INTO YOUR BODY.

FEEL YOURSELF FLOATING INTO YOURSELF.

DOWN TO THE THIGH ON YOUR RIGHT.

FEEL IT AND FLEX THE MUSCLE,

SLOWLY, AND THEN RELAX.

FLEX IT AGAIN; THEN STOP; CONCENTRATE ON THE THIGH.

GENTLY FLEX YOUR THIGH; FEEL THE PRESSURE JUST BACK OF THE KNEE;

FEEL THE UNDERSIDE OF YOUR KNEE.

FLEX AGAIN—AND FOCUS;

FEEL THE THIGH AGAINST THE CHAIR.

FLEX, AND RELAX—AND STOP.

~~~~~~~~~~~

Within each 60 seconds of feeling inward, move to another part of your body—ankle, calf, hip, chest, neck, etc. For each 60 seconds, focus all of your attention on one part, then move, stretch, flex, relax, push, pull, relax, push, relax, move, relax . . . Concentrate, feel inward, sense and experience your body. Become aware of the movement of a joint; sense the position of a bone; feel the rhythm of movement; feel the slight pressure on a muscle, then the relaxation.

Continue these exercises until you can comfortably and easily feel and get in touch with various parts of your body. If you have trouble sensing any particular area, stop, relax, and move on to another part. Then at some later point in time, relax, go back to that area, focus, concentrate, and exercise again. Don't push it; don't strain; let it come easily. Sense your way gradually, letting the impulses glide through your body. Be alert inwardly, but also assume your new-found experience of relaxed attention.

Gradually, as you continue to exercise, you will become acutely aware of the variety and fineness of internal stimuli you are now capable of experiencing. What was once unfelt will become vivid, clear, and distinct. The small pressures, the tiny movements, the subtle feelings of position and rhythm will come into focus; they are all part of you. You will discover the richness of internal sensations. It requires no special talent, no special ability or sensitivity. All of us are born with this kind of potential capacity for experiencing ourselves; it merely requires opening yourself—and the practice, the patience, the concentrated, focused attention inherent in the exercises will enlarge your awareness.

2 or 3
Minutes
at a Time

~~~~~~~~~~~~~~

In the 60-second breaks, the moments in between, you have begun to capture some of the subtleties of experience that all of us can know. In the waiting times of everyday life, you've used a moment now and then, stopped your blankness and started the process of growing awareness. There has been nothing esoteric, nothing strange or mysterious; as a matter of fact, you have simply learned to become aware of experience that is always *there*. And like most of the important things of life, it is really quite simple, if you know how to use time, focus your attention, break old sets of sensing and thinking, and gently live yourself into a new world of awareness.

It's like looking at a piece of sculpture, first from one view, then another, and another. New forms become apparent, new shapes, patterns, shadows. What was once only stone or metal takes on new life and meaning, and your world is deepened and enriched. So too we have asked you to sense your own world of experience, "walk" around yourself as you might walk around a piece of sculpture, gaining new perspectives and discovering new meanings. It has only been 60 seconds at a time, but the results have inevitably changed you, sharpened your senses, broken old sets, and expanded your capacity for awareness. With each 60-second exercise the growth is small and subtle; few great leaps or dramatic flashes. But if you have practiced, the growth has been sure, and you have begun to sense the potential within you.

We now offer some exercises that take from 2 to 3 minutes. Begin these only after you feel confident of your 60-second warm-ups, for they are the bases for future growth. And even though you move to the more complex and more demanding exercises, from time to time go back to the brief exercises, keeping your basic sensory skills sharpened and focused.

Up to this point we have stressed the value of freeing your consciousness from the limitations imposed by language. This was a most important part of the initial process of breaking old sets. But now that you've achieved the first level of growth, now that you have broken through the old sets guarded by words, you can use language to further expand your awareness. You are no longer the automatic, unthinking servant of your language, living within a shell of experience filtered by words, and now language can serve your own purposes for continued growth. Therefore, we believe that it will be helpful in the following exercises to keep some notes. Don't be at all concerned about logic or completeness; these aren't notes for some lecture or some examination. They're merely to help you remember your experiences, and with your remembering, you can recapture these experiences and build upon them for even more enriched awareness. Perhaps you'll only jot down a word, a phrase, anything that comes to mind; some reaction, some particular cue that seemed especially important, some thought about your own modification of an exercise. Nothing formal; nothing required. But when you feel like it, when it feels right, jot down a word or more, and then later, read, recall, and recapture the experience.

We will begin with some simpler exercises based directly on the 60-second warm-ups and then move to more complex levels of functioning. Remember to read each exercise twice before starting, and after you've done the exercise several times, reread the directions again. And, of course, as you practice, develop your own variations, your own styles.

Seeing Yourself (I)

You can do this now, if you have 2 minutes and a mirror—or wait till you find yourself in front of a mirror, washing your face, shaving, putting on lipstick, just looking.

MOVE TO ABOUT 4 TO 6 INCHES FROM THE MIRROR, AND LOOK AT YOUR EYES.

LOOK INTO YOUR EYES. FOCUS.

NOT TOO CLOSE. LOOK AT BOTH EYES AT THE SAME TIME.

CONCENTRATE INTO YOUR EYES.

STARE DIRECTLY, BUT RELAX.

LOOK, AND ASK YOURSELF "WHAT AM I AWARE OF?"

ATTEND TO YOUR FIRST FEELING, YOUR FIRST THOUGHT, YOUR FIRST PERCEPTION.

STAY WITH IT. FOCUS.

EXCLUDE ALL ELSE, AND BUILD THE INTENSITY OF THE EXPERIENCE.

TWO MINUTES ARE UP. STOP.

Two minutes more . . .

LOOK AND SEE INTO YOUR EYES. FOCUS.

SHIFT THE INTENSITY OF YOUR CONCENTRATION FROM ONE EYE TO THE OTHER.

FOCUS. SHIFT FROM ONE EYE TO THE OTHER.

NOW SEE INTO BOTH EYES—TOGETHER.

NOW TO ONE EYE;

TO THE OTHER.

MOVE FROM YOUR SEEING INTO YOUR EYES TO SEEING BETWEEN YOUR EYES, INTO THE PLACE BETWEEN YOUR EYES.

LOOK. FOCUS. SEE INTO THE SPACE BETWEEN YOUR EYES.

CONCENTRATE ON SEEING INTO THAT SPACE.

TWO MINUTES ARE UP. STOP. TWO MINUTES OF INTENSE, FOCUSED AWARENESS.

ENOUGH FOR NOW.

GO BACK TO WHATEVER YOU WERE DOING.

Seeing Yourself (II)

You're sitting in a bus or train, you're a passenger in a car, having a cup of coffee, tea, or waiting for a friend. You have 2 minutes, 2 minutes to see. Relax. Feel comfortable.

LOOK DOWN TO THE TIP OF YOUR NOSE. SLOWLY FOCUS.

CONCENTRATE. NOW STARE INTENSELY. FOCUS ON THE
TIP OF YOUR NOSE. BOTH EYES FOCUSING. SEEING. STOP.

NOW RELAX. KEEP ONE EYE OPEN; CLOSE THE OTHER,

AND FOCUS. LOOK TO THE TIP OF YOUR NOSE. SEE.

CONCENTRATE. RELAX. SLOWLY CLOSE BOTH EYES.

NOW REPEAT WITH THE OTHER EYE OPEN. FOCUS ON
THE TIP OF YOUR NOSE. STARE.

AFTER YOU'VE DONE THIS 3 TIMES, OPEN BOTH EYES.
FOCUS ON THE TIP OF YOUR NOSE. BOTH EYES LOOKING.
SEEING.

RELAX. CONCENTRATE ON FIXING AWARENESS AT THE TIP
OF YOUR NOSE. SEEING THE TIP.

NOW CLOSE BOTH EYES, AND IN YOUR MIND "SEE" THE
TIP OF YOUR NOSE AS YOU HAVE JUST SEEN IT.

STOP. TWO MINUTES ARE UP. RELAX. RETURN TO THE
EVERYDAY WORLD.

~~~~~~~~~~~

Practice. Calmly. Don't strain; don't rush. There is no
hurry, go slow. Relax.

Listening Within

Do you have 2 or 3 minutes free? In the morning before
you get out of bed? In the evening just before you are ready
to go to sleep? Turn off the radio, the television, the air
conditioner, anything else that is making noise. It is important to do this exercise in a quiet place because it involves listening to the sounds within your body. Lie flat on
your back. Take away all pillows, blankets, and covers. Let

your body assume a comfortable position. Breathe deeply, concentrate, and listen.

RELAX AND PRESS THE MIDDLE FINGER OF EACH HAND AGAINST YOUR EARS.

BLOCK OUT THE SOUNDS AROUND YOU.

CONCENTRATE AND LISTEN. LISTEN TO THE SOUNDS INSIDE OF YOU.

TRY TO EXCLUDE ALL OTHER SENSATIONS. DON'T THINK; FOCUS ON THE SOUNDS YOU HEAR, THE INTERNAL SOUNDS.

HEAR YOUR SOUND.

RELAX. NOW BREATHE IN THROUGH YOUR MOUTH. SLOWLY, SLOWLY.

HOLD YOUR BREATH AND LISTEN.

SLOWLY. RELAX. LISTEN.

FOCUS ON HEARING.

LISTEN. THE SOUND OF HUMMING.

CONCENTRATE AND STAY WITH THE SOUND YOU HEAR.

BREATHE OUT AND LISTEN. DOES THE SOUND CHANGE?

LISTEN. BREATHE IN THROUGH YOUR NOSE. HOLD IT.

HEAR THE SOUND—EXHALE.

BREATHE IN AND OUT, AND LISTEN. SWALLOW, AND FOCUS ON THE CHANGING SOUND.

STOP. TWO MINUTES ARE UP; RETURN TO WHAT YOU WERE DOING.

If you are uncomfortable blocking your ears with your fingers, or find that you cannot block out all external noises that way, use a small bit of cotton or earplugs to block your ears. And concentrate on your internal sounds. If you have sharpened your listening and hearing in the 60-second warm-ups, and external noises are fully blocked, you discover a remarkable world of sound inside of you. Concentrate and listen inward.

Breathing and Muscle Control

You're at home; it's quiet and you're alone. Your favorite chair or couch is inviting.

SIT DOWN AND RELAX. GET COMFORTABLE. BE NATURAL. SIT STRAIGHT BUT NOT STIFF. EASY.

FIRMLY PUT YOUR HANDS ON YOUR KNEES. RELAX.

NOW FIRMLY BUT GENTLY BREATHE OUT ALL OF YOUR AIR.

LET IT FLOW OUT.

AS YOU'RE BREATHING OUT, SLOWLY, EASILY CONTRACT THE MUSCLES OF YOUR ABDOMEN AND YOUR CHEST. PULL IN.

VERY SLOWLY PRESS YOUR HANDS FIRMLY AGAINST YOUR KNEES.

STRETCH YOUR NECK AND THE MUSCLES OF YOUR SHOULDERS. EASY. PRESS ON YOUR KNEES. GENTLY.

NOW BEGIN TO BREATHE IN, SLOWLY, VERY SLOWLY.

AND AT THE SAME TIME RELAX YOUR ABDOMINAL
MUSCLES. TAKE IN AIR. SLOWLY.

RELAX YOUR NECK AND SHOULDERS.

STOP PRESSING YOUR HANDS AGAINST YOUR KNEES, AND
SLOWLY INHALE, RELAXING YOUR ABDOMEN.

~~~~~~~~~~~~~

Repeat again—and again for your 2 to 3 minutes.

This complex exercise requires coordination and a great
deal of concentration. Doing it properly demands practice.
Don't rush it. Don't be impatient. At first, it will probably
seem awkward, and your experience is likely to be confused,
even uncomfortable. But with continued practice the different parts of the exercise will flow together, and through the
connection and unity you will discover a new sense of
awareness. Eventually the calm that follows this exercise
will last longer and longer.

Freeing Your Associations

The previous exercises concentrated on breaking old perceptual sets and developing new sensitivities to physical
stimulation: learning to see again, to hear again, to taste,
and touch, and sense your body from a new point of view,
a new perspective.

Now we turn to another mode of experience—language.
First, a word of caution. We began with sensory experiences
because it is easier to break old habits of experience, old
ways of sensing physical stimuli than to change the ways
we use language or the ways we think.

At a very young age, a tremendous amount of time and
effort is devoted to "conventionalizing" our use of language.

We are taught to speak the way everyone else does; we are taught to spell, to read, to write, to use the rules of grammar; in short, to use language according to the conventions of our society. Language conventions are very important, for without them—if everyone used language in his own idiosyncratic way—communication between people would be impossible. Without communication, no society could exist; and without a society, the human animal could not survive this world.

One result, however, of this "conventionalizing" is the constriction of our language. And since we think in words, it results also in the constriction of our thinking. If we are going to expand our capacity for consciousness in thinking, we will have to ignore some of the conventions of language.

A basic technique of psychoanalysis is free association. An analyst asks the patient to say whatever comes to mind, hoping in this way, to break through the conventions of language to an understanding of the patient's unconscious processes. We are not concerned here with understanding the unconscious, but rather with a similar free-association technique to expand the boundaries of language and free our thinking. In addition, by loosening up our word associations, we'll move away from the common connotations of word meaning into new forms of experience.

To begin this exercise, find a place where you can write without being disturbed. You'll need a pen or a pencil. Read the exercise twice and then turn to the "Freeing Your Associations" chart on page 109.

A QUIET PLACE, NO DISTRACTION.

NOW FOCUS ON THE PAPER;

DON'T LOOK AROUND; JUST LET YOUR MIND WANDER—
LET YOUR MIND WANDER TO WHEREVER IT TAKES YOU.

BEGIN LISTING IN THE FIRST COLUMN ANY WORDS AS
THEY OCCUR TO YOU.

THERE IS ONLY ONE RULE: DON'T WRITE PHRASES OR
SENTENCES; JUST WORDS.

EACH WORD YOU WRITE IN YOUR LIST SHOULD BE FREE
AND INDEPENDENT OF THE NEXT WORD.

KEEP GOING FOR 2 MINUTES. WRITE AS MANY WORDS
AS YOU CAN.

NOW STOP, CLOSE THE BOOK, AND PUT IT AWAY.

DON'T LOOK AT IT; DON'T THINK ABOUT IT.

GO BACK TO WHATEVER YOU WERE DOING BEFORE YOU
STARTED THIS EXERCISE.

Your next 2 minutes become available. Repeat exactly the
same exercise.

CONTINUE DOWN THE COLUMN, LISTING WORDS, ONE
AFTER ANOTHER.

REMEMBER, EACH WORD SHOULD BE INDEPENDENT OF
THE PRECEDING WORD.

LET YOUR MIND WANDER, BE FREE.

AND WHEN YOU FINISH A COLUMN ON THE FIRST PAGE,
TURN TO THE FIRST COLUMN OF THE NEXT PAGE.

CONTINUE FOR 2 TO 3 MINUTES—AS LONG AS THE WORDS
FLOW.

NOW STOP.

DON'T THINK ABOUT THE WORDS BETWEEN EXERCISES.

JUST GO ABOUT DOING WHAT YOU ORDINARILY WOULD
DO.

The next 2 to 3 minutes.

LOOK AT THE FIRST WORD YOU WROTE, AND BEGINNING WITH THAT FIRST WORD, AS QUICKLY AS YOU CAN, AND WITHOUT THINKING, WITHOUT PONDERING, WRITE DOWN THE FIRST WORD THAT COMES TO MIND.

WRITE IT DOWN IN THE SECOND COLUMN.

DON'T WORRY ABOUT MAKING SENSE; DON'T THINK ABOUT IT.

BE SPONTANEOUS; THE LESS OBVIOUS SENSE THERE IS, THE FREER YOU ARE BECOMING.

CONTINUE WITH THE SECOND WORD IN THE FIRST COLUMN.

SAY IT TO YOURSELF, THEN WRITE DOWN THE FIRST WORD THAT COMES TO MIND—RIGHT NEXT TO IT.

THE VERY FIRST IMPRESSION IS WHAT COUNTS.

CONTINUE IN THIS WAY FOR 2 MINUTES, WRITING ONE WORD NEXT TO EACH WORD IN YOUR FIRST LIST.

GO AS RAPIDLY AS YOU CAN.

DON'T FIGURE THEM OUT.

STAY LOOSE, FREE.

STOP.

When you have another 2 minutes . . .

GO BACK TO YOUR WORDS, AND CONTINUE TO WRITE YOUR ASSOCIATIONS TO EVERY WORD IN YOUR FIRST COLUMN.

YOU HAVE NOW WRITTEN 2 COLUMNS OF WORDS NEXT TO EACH OTHER.

BEGIN WITH THE WORD AT THE TOP OF THE SECOND COLUMN,

AND IN THE THIRD COLUMN CONTINUE AS BEFORE, WRITING YOUR IMMEDIATE ASSOCIATIONS TO EACH WORD.

WORK AS QUICKLY AS YOU CAN: THE FIRST WORD THAT YOU THINK OF—ANY WORD, NO MATTER WHAT—WRITE IT;

MOVE ON TO THE NEXT WORD, WRITE;

MOVE ON TO THE NEXT, WRITE; THE NEXT AND THE NEXT.

PICK UP THE PACE.

FASTER.

TWO MINUTES ARE UP.
STOP.

Continue this exercise, going as rapidly as you can until you maintain a fast, steady pace for the entire 2 minutes. Every once in a while, check your list to make sure you are not making "sensible" phrases or sentences. Repeat this exercise until you can keep the rapid, unbroken rhythm of associations for 2 minutes without falling into conventional phrases. Keep your associations original, novel, independent. Let your language go; free up your habits of verbal association 2 minutes at a time.

Chaining Your Associations

In the preceding exercise, you made one association to each word. In this exercise, we change the process a bit to strengthen your capacity for continuous associations.

You have 2 minutes to open up your awareness. Now look at the lists of words you've written for the previous exercise. Select one word at random. Don't think about it; just scan the lists and select the first word your eye stops at.

NOW CONCENTRATE. SAY THAT WORD TO YOURSELF, AND THEN

IMMEDIATELY ASSOCIATE ANOTHER WORD—THEN ANOTHER, AND ANOTHER,

REMEMBER: NO PHRASES, NO SENTENCES, JUST WORDS.

DON'T MAKE IT LOGICAL, DON'T TRY TO INJECT MEANING, AND DON'T ANALYZE.

JUST ASSOCIATE ONE WORD TO ANOTHER.

DON'T BOTHER WRITING THE WORDS; JUST SAY THEM TO YOURSELF.

CONTINUE FOR 2 MINUTES, AND THEN STOP.

Again for 2 or 3 minutes . . .

SELECT ANOTHER WORD FROM YOUR ORIGINAL LISTS.

SAY IT TO YOURSELF AND THEN

ASSOCIATE ANOTHER WORD TO THE FIRST; ANOTHER WORD TO THE SECOND—

ANOTHER, ANOTHER, AND ANOTHER FOR 2 MINUTES. STOP.

Continue this exercise until you can chain associations for 2 minutes without any appreciable pauses. If your associations begin to hang together in any obviously meaningful way, stop at once. Get another word from the list and start over again, chaining associations one after another without trying to make rational, logical sense.

A seemingly simple exercise? Perhaps—but one of the most difficult attempted thus far. It runs directly counter to a lifetime of chaining words in conventionally meaningful phrases and sentences. Here, we ask you to break those thoroughly over-learned habits and put words together in nonconventional, nonmeaningful chains. It's not a simple task done easily, comfortably, freely, with a steady, rhythmic pace, and a sense of flowing. So practice this exercise over and over again. It may take days—weeks—perhaps even longer to finally achieve the easy flow we're after, but the steady practice is well worth the time and effort. You will gain a verbal freedom and fluency you have never experienced before, and the powers of your mind will be enormously expanded.

Satiating Your Associations

Now we'll try something new with your associations. You should have little problem by now doing the freeing and chaining association exercises.

Again, find a quiet place where you'll be comfortable and undisturbed. Get a pen or pencil. Look back at the lists of words you wrote. As your eye seems to land on one of the words from the list—remember it. Turn to "Satiating Your Associations" on page 111 and write *that* word down at the top of Column 1.

CONCENTRATE AND FOCUS ON THAT SINGLE WORD; THEN CONTINUE WRITING THE SAME WORD—OVER AND OVER AGAIN IN COLUMN 1.

AS YOU WRITE THE WORD, SAY IT TO YOURSELF.

WRITE THE WORD OVER AND OVER AGAIN.

SAY IT. ATTEND TO THE WORD EACH TIME YOU WRITE IT.

WRITE IT. SAY IT. AGAIN—

WRITE IT, SAY IT, AGAIN AND AGAIN.

KEEP ON FOCUSING ON THE WORD—FILL UP COLUMN 1 WRITING THE SAME WORD.

NOW STOP—WHAT'S THE FIRST WORD THAT COMES TO YOUR MIND?

WRITE DOWN THE VERY FIRST WORD THAT COMES TO YOUR MIND, AT THE TOP OF COLUMN 2.

CLOSE THE BOOK AND RETURN TO WHAT YOU WERE DOING. DON'T THINK ABOUT THE WORDS.

Another 2 minutes . . .

TURN BACK TO THE PAGE WHERE YOU WROTE THE FIRST WORD;

LOOK AT THE WORD YOU WROTE ON THE TOP OF COLUMN 2. SAY THE WORD ALOUD.

WRITE IT. SAY IT—AS BEFORE.

WRITE IT. KEEP ON WRITING IT AND SAYING IT, SAYING IT AND WRITING IT, WITHOUT STOPPING.

CONCENTRATE ON SAYING AND WRITING. DON'T THINK

ABOUT IT. FILL IN ALL THE LINES IN COLUMN 2, AND
THEN STOP.

NOW WHAT'S THE FIRST WORD YOU THINK OF?

WRITE IT IN AT THE TOP OF COLUMN 3, AND THEN STOP.

Another 2 minutes become available . . .

LOOK AT THE WORD ON TOP OF COLUMN 3. SAY IT
ALOUD; WRITE IT.

SAY THE SAME WORD AGAIN AND WRITE IT.

FILL UP ALL THE LINES IN COLUMN 3.

NOW LOOK AT YOUR ASSOCIATIONS. ARE THEY COMMON
ONES? ARE THEY WORDS THAT YOU MIGHT ORDINARILY
ASSOCIATE WITH THE FIRST WORD?

~~~~~~~~~~~

This satiation exercise obviously demands an almost automatic routine in which you repeat the same response over
and over again. It is simple, mechanical, repetitive; yet it is
a most effective way of loosening and freeing your associations. Thus, if you are having any trouble freeing or chaining associations for the preceding exercises, try a few 2- to
3-minute sessions of satiation. You are likely to discover that
you can go back to the free-association or chained-association
exercises with an enhanced flexibility and fluency. The
satiation exercise is mechanical, but it can have a very
powerful effect.

You have now practiced three of the basic verbal association exercises: Freeing Your Associations, Chaining Your
Associations, and Satiating Your Associations. Don't be
disturbed if the exercises are difficult for you in the beginning. The habits of language usage are so well learned

and so thoroughly practiced that it is hard to escape from the verbal ruts and the rigidity we have built for ourselves. It's most important that you be consistent in your practice of the exercises, keeping your inner ear peeled for sequences that begin to "make sense." As soon as you realize you have fallen into one of these ruts, stop, relax, and begin again, remaining as loose as possible, and keeping your associations free and flowing. As you practice, you will gradually notice your skill improving; you will feel less blocked, the chain of associations will be more fluid, you will experience a kind of verbal dance in which you can freely play with words in an easy, joyful way. Your associations will be freer, more individual, more *you.*

Don't expect to develop this capacity all at once. Remember how many years you have spent learning and using the conventions of language and thought. The capacity to escape from these conventions develops gradually, with practice, but when you have acquired this ability, continue to practice and strengthen it. You have learned one of the basic cognitive skills underlying many other methods of mind expansion.

Shifting Perspectives

We move now to a different level of psychic functioning, requiring a readiness to let yourself go imaginatively, but with flexible control.

In our introduction, we emphasized the idea of perception and perceptual sets. We noted that perception always involves some point of view, some perspective from which each of us perceives the world and ourselves, and we discussed the need to develop capacities to shift and change from our usual perspectives of everyday life. This exercise is designed to multiply the vantage points from which we experience the world.

You can do this exercise as you're waiting on line in a store, a post office, waiting to get into a theater, or in your doctor's office or at the beauty parlor or barber shop. Whenever 2 minutes become available.

SLOWLY LOOK AROUND YOU—ALL AROUND, UP AND DOWN, SIDEWAYS.

NOW IMAGINE YOURSELF LOOKING AT THE SAME SCENE AS IF YOU WERE 20 FEET UP IN THE AIR.

YOU HAVE SHIFTED POSITION, SHIFTED PERSPECTIVE.

IMAGINE HOW THINGS LOOK FROM UP ABOVE.

FOCUS ON ONE OBJECT. ANYTHING—A CHAIR, A BOX.

NOW IMAGINE YOURSELF ABOVE IT. WHAT DOES IT LOOK LIKE?

HOW DOES IT CHANGE AS YOU MOVE?

YOU'RE RIGHT ABOVE IT.

SCAN THE WHOLE SCENE FROM ABOVE.

CLOSE YOUR EYES. PICTURE IT. IMAGINE HOW IT MUST LOOK.

DOES THE LIGHT CHANGE? ARE THERE SHADOWS? ARE THERE PEOPLE? IF SO, CAN YOU SEE THE TOPS OF THEIR HEADS?

IMAGINE. PICTURE IT TO YOURSELF. VISUALIZE IT.

NOW STOP. COME BACK. ENOUGH.

Could you shift? Did you picture the entire scene from above? Did you see everything you wanted to see? Probably not this first time. So find another 2 minutes in between, another break. Same setting.

LOOK AROUND. SHIFT PERSPECTIVE. UP ABOVE.

MOVE YOUR POINT OF VIEW UP, AND THEN LOOK DOWN.

LOOK AT YOURSELF. IMAGINE IT.

HOW DO YOU LOOK? PICTURE IT.

EASIER THIS TIME? EASIER TO SHIFT, TO SEE THINGS FROM ABOVE? TO SEE YOURSELF?

LOOK DOWN. SCAN. FOCUS.

WATCH THE DETAILS. PICK OUT AN OBJECT. LOOK AT IT FROM UP ABOVE.

TWO MINUTES. STOP. GO BACK TO WHERE YOU WERE.

Another 2 minutes become available . . . This time, a new perspective.

IMAGINE YOURSELF LOOKING UP FROM YOUR FEET.

LOOK UP.

HOW DOES THE WORLD CHANGE?

WHAT DO YOU SEE THAT YOU DID NOT SEE BEFORE?

WHERE ARE THE TABLES, THE CHAIRS? HOW DO THEY LOOK?

IMAGINE IT. PICTURE IT. HOLD THE PERSPECTIVE.

NOW SCAN. MOVE AROUND. SCAN.

HOLD IT.

STOP. GO BACK TO YOUR NORMAL PERSPECTIVE.

Again—2 minutes free . . .

> SHIFT PERSPECTIVE. DOWN.
>
> LOOK UP FROM YOUR FOOT.
>
> SCAN. FOCUS ON ONE OBJECT. IMAGINE WHAT IT LOOKS LIKE FROM BELOW.
>
> PICK OUT THE DETAILS.
>
> FOCUS. PICTURE IT. THE LIGHTING, THE SHADOWS, THE SHAPE. COLORS.
>
> DO THEY CHANGE? HOLD IT. SCAN.
>
> STOP. GO BACK TO NORMAL.

———————————

At first, it may be very difficult to achieve these shifts. We are so used to seeing the world from our own perspective that it is hard to imaginatively shift our views. During your first few tries, you may get only a glimpse, a momentary shift. Don't rush it. Don't worry about it. Be satisfied with that moment. It will grow. Practice imaginative shifting. You don't need to be anywhere special. Sitting at a table, standing in line, walking down a street, anywhere. Shift your perspective, move it up, further up, way up—15, 20, 30 feet. Move it down to waist level, to knee level, to the ground. Can you imagine your eyes being located in these different positions? See it. What does the world look like?

Gradually, your imaginative capacity will expand, grow stronger, surer, more flexible. And as your ability to shift perspectives is enhanced, you will discover the excitement of viewing old scenes from new vantage points. Settings you have been in a thousand times will take on added richness, with new forms, new patterns you have never seen before.

Finding You in Yourself

In the preceding exercise you developed your ability to shift perspectives in your views of the external world. Now we shall focus inward again, practicing a different kind of shifting perspective.

You may not have realized it before, but everyone experiences himself at some specific point in his body. In one sense, of course, we *are* our bodies; my little toe on my left foot is no less *me* than my head or chest. But psychologically, each of us feels "localized" in some particular spot, some specific area of the body. Different people experience themselves in different places, and of course, there is no right place, no normal place—just *your* place—the place in yourself where you feel you are.

It's morning and you're getting up for the day, or it's evening, the busy day is over and you've got 2 minutes free.

QUIET; RELAX; WITHDRAW INTO YOURSELF. FOCUS AND CONCENTRATE.

WHERE ARE YOU IN YOUR BODY?

FIND YOU IN YOUR BODY. FEEL IT. EXPERIENCE IT. LET IT COME.

SLOWLY; EASILY; FEEL IT. CONCENTRATE. GOT IT? HOLD IT.

STOP. RETURN TO WHAT YOU WERE DOING.

Don't try to make sense of this. Don't try to figure it out, explain it. And don't make up some spot in your body that sounds rational and reasonable. It doesn't matter where the spot is, just experience it without thinking about it.

Another 2-minute break . . .

> STOP AND RELAX. WITHDRAW INTO YOURSELF.
>
> CONCENTRATE. FORGET EVERYTHING ELSE IN THE WORLD. FOCUS ENTIRELY ON YOURSELF.
>
> WHERE ARE YOU?
>
> FLOW INTO THAT SPOT. FEEL IT? SURE? EXPERIENCE IT. PINPOINT IT. FOCUS ON IT. IMAGINE IT. FOCUS.
>
> GOT IT? CONCENTRATE. FOCUS.
>
> STOP.

Another 2 minutes . . .

> WITHDRAW INTO YOURSELF.
> RELAX. FOCUS ON WHERE YOU ARE IN YOUR BODY.
>
> SLOWLY, GRADUALLY MOVE YOURSELF DOWN.
>
> IMAGINE IT. PICTURE IT. FEEL YOURSELF MOVING, FLOWING, SLOWLY DOWN THROUGH YOUR BODY.
>
> SLOWLY DOWN. HOLD IT. STOP.
>
> WHERE ARE YOU?
>
> FEEL IT.
>
> NOW, SLOWLY, BACK UP, UP SLOWLY, BACK.
>
> STOP. HOLD IT.

Again, 2 minutes . . .

> FOCUS ON WHERE YOU ARE IN YOUR BODY.
>
> MOVE YOURSELF OUT ALONG YOUR ARM.
>
> CONCENTRATE. IMAGINE. SLOWLY—THROUGH THE WRIST. THROUGH THE PALM. INTO THE FINGERS.

HOLD IT.

BACK. SLOW. EASY. BACK UP THROUGH YOUR ARM.

HOLD IT. FOCUS. STOP.

Again, 2 minutes . . .

FOCUS.
MOVE YOURSELF THROUGH YOUR BODY.

SLOWLY. LET YOURSELF GLIDE.

EASY. SETTLE. REST.

EXPERIENCE YOURSELF IN THIS NEW POSITION.

NOW MOVE YOURSELF. MOVE. ANYWHERE.

FOCUS. MOVE BACK; BACK TO NORMAL. BACK.

STOP. RELAX.

――――――――――

This is probably the most difficult exercise we have described up to this point. It requires great concentration—withdrawing into yourself, focusing, and then paying attention and sensing yourself in your body, imaginatively shifting and moving throughout your body. Don't try this exercise until you have some sense of mastery of the preceding exercises, particularly the basic sensory and associative ones. After you have achieved a comfortable level of skill in these earlier exercises, it will be easier. Try shifting perspectives and moving yourself. Maintain a light, easy, playful mood. Don't get somber, serious, heavy, dull. *Play* with this exercise. Smile and try it. If you find you can't do it, drop it. Forget it. Then come back again another time, another day. You have to catch yourself in the right mood, the right frame of mind. Don't try to define it. You will know when it happens, and once you get it, it will click, and you will be able to exercise almost anytime you like—with a new sense of awareness.

Drawing Open Circles

Whenever you have 2 minutes, some unlined paper and a pen or pencil, sit comfortably at a table or desk. Relax.

START SLOWLY DRAWING SMALL CIRCLES.

ONE, TWO, THREE. CONTINUE TO DRAW CIRCLES.

MAKE THE CIRCLES OPEN, EASY. SLOWLY. AUTO-MATICALLY.

MAKE SMALL OPEN CIRCLES, FILLING UP THE WHOLE PAGE, MOVING FROM LEFT TO RIGHT.

RELAX. CONCENTRATE ON MAKING THE CIRCLES VERY CLOSE TOGETHER, YET NOT TOUCHING.

SLOWLY. START FROM THE LEFT-HAND CORNER.

MAKE A LINE OF CIRCLES, AS YOU WOULD IF YOU WERE WRITING. FOCUS AND CONCENTRATE.

THEN START ANOTHER LINE.

CONCENTRATE. FOCUS YOUR ATTENTION ONLY ON THE CIRCLES, THE OPEN CIRCLES.

DO IT SLOWLY AT FIRST.

MAKE ANOTHER LINE. NOW START MAKING THE CIRCLES FASTER. KEEP ON MAKING CIRCLES—AUTOMATICALLY—FOCUS. FILL UP THE PAGE.

IF YOU HAVE MORE THAN 2 MINUTES, START ANOTHER
PAGE.

NOW SLOW DOWN. DRAW THE CIRCLES EVEN MORE
SLOWLY.

OPEN CIRCLES—CONCENTRATE AND LET YOUR AWARE-
NESS FOCUS ON THE CIRCLES.

NOW SHIFT BACK TO DRAWING THEM FASTER.

ROWS OF SMALL OPEN CIRCLES.

WHAT WERE YOU AWARE OF?

STOP.

~~~~~~~~~~~~

Seeing People—and Yourself

People-watching has always been a fascinating pastime.
Everybody enjoys looking at other people. Let's see if we
can become more aware not only of the fun of it, but of
its value as a means of expanding consciousness.

This exercise may be done in trains, subways, buses, class-
rooms, etc. Wherever and whenever you find yourself in a
situation where you're facing someone who is not aware of
your presence. Feel comfortable. Friendly. Relax. Try to
look at the other person and really see him or her. Dis-
creetly, concentrate and focus your complete attention on
the other person.

SLOWLY. IN A FRIENDLY WAY. LOOK AT EACH OF THE
SPECIFIC PARTS OF THE PERSON'S FACE.

BECOME AWARE OF ALL THE DETAILS.

SEE THE COLOR, THE TONE, THE SHAPE, CURVES, TEX-
TURE AND LINES OF THE PERSON'S FACE.

FOCUS. WHAT EXPRESSION IS ON THE FACE? WHAT
PARTS OF THE FACE MOVE?

RELAX. BECOME AWARE OF CHANGES IN YOUR AWARE-
NESS OF THE FACE.

FOCUS ON THE CHANGES THAT YOU SEE.

HOW DOES THE PERSON SEEM TO FEEL?

NOW CLOSE YOUR EYES.

SLOWLY, CONCENTRATE. SEE A PICTURE OF YOUR FACE.
FOCUS IN ON YOUR OWN SENSE OF HOW YOU LOOK.

FOCUS YOUR ATTENTION. CONCENTRATE AND VISUALIZE
YOUR FACE WITH YOUR EYES CLOSED.

HOW DOES YOUR FACE LOOK—ITS COLOR, SHAPE,
CURVES?

RELAX. FOCUS IN ON YOUR OWN FACE. BECOME AWARE
OF YOUR OWN FACE AND ITS SPECIFIC FEATURES.

HOW DOES IT APPEAR?

CONCENTRATE ON YOUR IMAGE OF YOUR FACE.

NOW OPEN YOUR EYES.

SLOWLY, LOOK AT THE OTHER PERSON'S FACE. LET THE
OTHER PERSON'S FACE APPEAR AGAIN.

SEE IT. FIX YOUR ATTENTION ON THE DETAILS OF THE
OTHER PERSON'S FEATURES.

CONCENTRATE. FEEL FRIENDLY.

HOW DIFFERENT DOES HE LOOK? WHAT HAVE YOU BE-
COME AWARE OF?

RELAX. STOP.

You're on your way into your new-found sense of awareness. If you have gone through and practiced the 60-second warm-up exercises and dipped into the 2- to 3-minute exercises, you've experienced a new sensation of consciousness, a sense that there is a new world of experience out there and also inside you. The taste of previous exercises should have succeeded in whetting your appetite—alerting you that there could be more—getting you ready for further awakening and expansion of your awareness. In the following exercises, try to begin using the notes you've made of your experience. Spend a few minutes looking them over—see how you've opened your feelings. Remember, don't let the note-taking interfere with the exercises, but when you finish an exercise, just try to jot down something about the experience—whether it is a word that represents a feeling or a sentence, or a drawing—anything that impressed you about your awareness of consciousness.

Feeling and Seeing

Let's continue to get into our consciousness. Slowly, concentrate and focus quietly—absorbing your experience of awareness in detail. Let go—let yourself go by opening up your awareness, surrender to your fantasy and your reality; their interaction will bring about a new experience of pleasurable growth and wholeness.

You have 2 to 3 minutes free . . .

WALK SLOWLY TO A MIRROR—LOOK AT YOUR FACE.

WHAT DO YOU SEE? ANYTHING UNUSUAL?

WHAT ARE YOU FEELING?

NOW CLOSE YOUR EYES, GENTLY. RELAX.

CONCENTRATE. THINK OF SOMETHING THAT MAKES YOU ANGRY OR HAS RECENTLY MADE YOU ANGRY.

GET ANGRY, BUT KEEP YOUR EYES CLOSED. FEEL ANGRY— VERY ANGRY.

LET YOURSELF FEEL THE ANGER. CONCENTRATE ON FEELING ANGRY.

FOCUS ON OPENING UP AND LETTING YOURSELF FEEL THE ANGER THROUGHOUT YOUR WHOLE BODY.

LET IT BUILD. FEEL THE ANGER.

OPEN YOUR EYES—LOOK INTO THE MIRROR.

LOOK AT YOUR FACE. LOOK INTO YOUR EXPRESSION— THE LINES ON YOUR FACE, YOUR LIPS, YOUR EYES, THE POSITION OF YOUR HEAD.

HOW DO YOU LOOK? IS IT A DIFFERENT LOOK—DIF- FERENT FROM THE WAY YOU LOOKED BEFORE?

STOP.

Two to three minutes again.

RELAX, TAKE IT EASY. FEEL COMFORTABLE, FEEL GOOD, AND LET YOURSELF FEEL HAPPY.

WALK TO THE MIRROR.

CLOSE YOUR EYES.

THINK OF A RECENT EXPERIENCE THAT MADE YOU FEEL HAPPY.

FEEL IT. LET THE HAPPY FEELING SPREAD THROUGH YOUR BODY.

WHAT IS THAT EXPERIENCE? FEEL IT. EXPERIENCE IT. FOCUS.

CONCENTRATE ON THE EXPERIENCE OF HAPPINESS—LET YOURSELF INTO IT; OPEN YOURSELF TO THE FEELING.

NOW OPEN YOUR EYES. LOOK INTO THE MIRROR.

HOW DO YOU LOOK? WHAT IS THE EXPRESSION ON YOUR FACE—THE LINES, THE CONTOURS? YOUR LIPS? YOUR EYES.

LOOK; FOCUS; STOP.

~~~~~~~~~~~~

You might try this exercise with other feelings—sadness, fear, love. In only 2 minutes of empty time, you can become more aware of how your feelings are reflected in your face, how the rest of the world sees you when you're angry or loving, happy or sad.

Becoming More a Part of the World

Try the following exercise over and over again whenever you have 2 to 3 minutes. Practice *becoming* the thing you let your mind wander to. Let yourself *experience* identity. Try to become the object, to feel what it is like to *be* it.

LET YOUR AWARENESS WANDER.

RELAX AND WANDER. SEE WHERE IT TAKES YOU.

SEE WHERE YOUR IMAGINATION TAKES YOU.

RELAX. WHAT STANDS OUT?

FOCUS IN ON WHAT IS EMERGING.

CONCENTRATE ON WHAT IS EMERGING.

WHAT IS IT? MOVE INTO IT. FOCUS. ATTEND.

BECOME AWARE OF THE DETAILS—WHAT IS IT?

WHAT DOES IT LOOK LIKE? WHAT DOES IT FEEL LIKE?

NOW, BECOME IT—WHATEVER IT IS. FLOW INTO IT.

IF IT'S A COLOR, FEEL THAT COLOR; AN OBJECT, LET YOURSELF FEEL LIKE THAT OBJECT. SLOWLY BECOME THAT OBJECT.

WHAT ARE YOU LIKE? EXPERIENCE IT.

TRY TO SAY SILENTLY, QUIETLY, TO YOURSELF THAT YOU ARE THIS THING.

VISUALIZE YOURSELF AS THE OBJECT.

DON'T THINK ABOUT IT. FEEL IT. JUST LET YOURSELF FEEL LIKE YOU'RE THE OBJECT.

STAY WITH IT. RELAX. CONCENTRATE. LET YOURSELF BECOME AWARE OF HOW IT FEELS TO BE WHATEVER IT WAS THAT YOUR MIND WANDERED TO.

CONCENTRATE.

FOCUS ON THE OBJECT. STOP.

~~~~~~~~~~~~~~~

How did you feel? Did you *feel* your experience? Were you aware of yourself as that thing? Was it a physical feeling? How did you feel this change in awareness? Try to write down something of your experience.

Another Look at Yourself

Get comfortable—in a quiet setting without distraction. You could either be sitting in a comfortable chair or lying on your back. The important thing is to feel relaxed. Close your eyes. Relax. Feel comfortable. Relax.

NOW IMAGINE YOURSELF AS AN AIRPLANE.

SEE YOURSELF AS AN AIRPLANE. FOCUS ON THE FEELING.

CONCENTRATE. FEEL AND SEE YOURSELF FLYING IN THE AIR LIKE AN AIRPLANE. FLOATING, GLIDING IN THE CLEAR SKY.

YOU ARE A PLANE. LET YOURSELF BECOME AWARE OF HOW IT FEELS TO BE FLOATING AND GLIDING ALONG IN THE SKY.

AS YOU'RE FLYING ALONG, RELAX. COMFORTABLE. LOOK DOWN. LOOK DOWN AT YOUR HOUSE.

HOW DOES IT LOOK? THE BUILDING.

LOOK INSIDE THE HOUSE—YOUR ROOM.

TURN YOUR ATTENTION TO YOURSELF. YOU ARE LOOKING AT YOURSELF FROM ABOVE. SEE YOURSELF.

RELAX. LOOK AT YOURSELF. FOCUS ON LOOKING AT YOURSELF. NOTICE WHAT YOU SEE.

HOW DO YOU FEEL LOOKING AT YOURSELF?

WHAT ARE YOUR THOUGHTS? IMAGES?

CONCENTRATE ON LOOKING AT YOURSELF. FEEL IT?

WHAT COMES INTO YOUR MIND? BECOME AWARE OF

WHAT YOU ARE FEELING AS YOU LOOK AT YOURSELF. RELAX. STAY WITH IT.

NOW SEE YOURSELF MOVE. FEEL IT. WHERE DID YOU MOVE? CONCENTRATE. HOW DID IT FEEL?

STOP. TWO MINUTES ARE UP. OPEN YOUR EYES.

WHAT DID YOU EXPERIENCE? WHAT WERE YOU AWARE OF?

~~~~~~~~~~~~~

You and Your Other Self

Here's another 2- to 3-minute break. This exercise is a variation on and flows out of the preceding one. It can be done sitting or lying comfortably. Relax. Experience yourself. The wholeness of yourself. The moments of sensing the present in yourself.

CLOSE YOUR EYES. CONCENTRATE ON EMPTYING YOUR MIND.

GET RID OF ALL THOSE THOUGHTS, IDEAS, WORDS— BREAK SET.

GET IN TOUCH MORE AND MORE WITH YOUR FLOWING FEELINGS OF THE MOMENT.

FOCUS IN ON YOURSELF. RELAX.

IMAGINE YOU ARE SITTING OPPOSITE YOURSELF. CON- CENTRATE AND SEE YOURSELF LOOKING AT YOU. VIS- UALIZE YOURSELF SITTING OPPOSITE YOU.

SEE YOURSELF AS IF YOU WERE LOOKING IN A MIRROR.

FOCUS. CAN YOU SEE YOURSELF? ATTEND.

HOW DO YOU LOOK? HOW ARE YOU SITTING?

BECOME AWARE OF YOU—LOOKING AT YOURSELF. SEE WHAT YOU ARE WEARING. CONCENTRATE.

WHAT EXPRESSION DO YOU HAVE ON YOUR FACE? HOW DO YOU FEEL? RELAX.

TELL YOURSELF ALOUD THE FIRST THING THAT COMES INTO YOUR MIND.

LISTEN. HOW DOES YOUR VOICE SOUND?

BECOME AWARE OF HOW YOU FEEL.

SHIFT TO THE OTHER YOU. BECOME THE OTHER YOU. RESPOND TO WHAT YOU SAID. ANSWER.

CONCENTRATE AND FOCUS ON WHAT YOU'RE SAYING AS THE OTHER YOU.

LISTEN. WHAT DID YOU SAY? FOCUS.

ANSWER YOURSELF. LISTEN. NOTICE WHAT YOU HAVE SAID.

ATTEND TO THE DETAILS OF LISTENING TO YOUR WORDS. THE FEELINGS.

HOW DID YOU FEEL RESPONDING TO YOURSELF?

NOW SWITCH BACK TO YOUR FORMER SELF.

SEE YOURSELF. CONCENTRATE.

WHAT ARE YOU FEELING?

SWITCH BACK AGAIN TO THE OTHER YOU. SAY WHAT'S ON YOUR MIND. LISTEN TO YOURSELF. CONCENTRATE.

FEEL THE EXPERIENCE OF WHAT YOU ARE SAYING.

STOP. OPEN YOUR EYES.

10
to 20
Minutes

~~~~~~~~~~~~~~~~~

Reliving Emotions

In this exercise, you will have an opportunity to call into play all of the basic skills you have developed in the preceding exercises. It is a complex task, but as you continue to practice, you will notice that each experience will be richer and somewhat easier than the last.

To some degree, we are always in a state of emotion. That is, we are always experiencing some degree of pleasantness/ unpleasantness, aliveness/deadness, some minimal awareness of a tone of feeling that might be perceived as emotional. But by and large, these feelings are so slight, so close to a neutral steady state, that we are unaware of their emotional dimension. We feel and label our experiences as emotional only when our reactions are intense and dramatic enough to break through the layer of psychological insulation that normally surrounds us. It is only then that we clearly recognize ourselves as feeling angry or loving, happy or sad, excited or bored.

This insulation, of course, has considerable functional and pragmatic value, for if we were constantly aware of our emotional state, the practical problem-solving aspects of everyday life would inevitably suffer. Our attention would be taken up by the pangs of anxiety or the bubbling feelings of joy rather than the external demands of driving a car, typing a letter, or doing any of the other hundreds of practical tasks that comprise our everyday lives.

Thus, we live most of our lives psychologically insulated from the more subtle aspects of our own emotional experience. And while that may be necessary in a society focused primarily on external doing, it is also psychologically deadening. Sometimes the insulation grows so thick that we live cushioned in an experiential world of bland neutrality—isolated from ourselves and our own feelings. Poets and philosophers have written sensitively of this blandness, ennui, and alienation as a major problem confronting man in Western society. This exercise, then, is designed to recapture some of the emotional sensitivity that almost all of us have had during the process of growing up, before the pragmatic pressures and the layers of civilized insulation grew too thick—and alienated our sense of feeling.

To begin, find a place where you won't be interrupted for the 10 to 20 minutes that will be necessary for this exercise. It should be a quiet, comfortable place.

RELAX. THEN TURN INWARD. CONCENTRATE.

THINK OF ONE SPECIFIC, CONCRETE, PARTICULAR TIME YOU FELT A STRONG EMOTION.

MOST PEOPLE FIND IT EASIEST IN THE BEGINNING TO THINK OF AN INSTANCE IN WHICH THEY FELT ANGRY, PERHAPS BECAUSE OUR FEELINGS OF ANGER TEND TO BE SOMEWHAT SHARPER, MORE DISTINCT THAN SOME OTHER EMOTIONAL STATES.

BUT IT DOESN'T MATTER WHAT EMOTIONAL STATE YOU CHOOSE,

JUST SO LONG AS YOU SELECT ONE SPECIFIC INSTANCE OF A STRONG AND INTENSE EMOTIONAL EXPERIENCE.

NOW THINK OF THE SITUATION YOU WERE IN AT THE TIME YOU EXPERIENCED THIS EMOTION.

VISUALIZE THE SETTING.

CAN YOU SEE IT? CONCENTRATE. SEE IT.

WHERE WERE YOU? WHAT WERE YOUR SURROUNDINGS?

IN A ROOM? WERE YOU OUTSIDE?

RECALL THE PHYSICAL OBJECTS THAT WERE THERE, THE PARTICULAR SHAPES, COLORS, TEXTURES. SEE THE DETAILS.

REMEMBER YOURSELF IN THE PHYSICAL SETTING.

WHAT WERE YOU DOING? WAS THERE ANOTHER PERSON PRESENT? WHAT DID THE OTHER PERSON LOOK LIKE? CONCENTRATE.

WHAT DID THE OTHER PERSON DO? WHAT DID THE OTHER PERSON SAY?

REMEMBER. IMAGINE YOURSELF FULLY, COMPLETELY, INTO THE SITUATION.

AND THEN YOU FELT SOMETHING.

WHERE? IN THE MUSCLES? IN YOUR THROAT? YOUR CHEST?

FOCUS INWARD; RECAPTURE YOUR FEELINGS; SENSE THEM; RE-SENSE THEM. SEE YOURSELF FEELING.

WAS IT HEAVY OR LIGHT? WAS IT SHARP OR DULL? FEEL IT.

WAS IT ACTIVE OR PASSIVE? DID IT FEEL FULL OR EMPTY? WAS IT FAST OR SLOW?

REMEMBER. RELIVE THE EMOTION. FEEL IT—AND FEEL YOURSELF FEELING IT.

LET YOURSELF GO; LET YOUR BODY GO—GET INTO THE FEELING, STOP ANALYZING—JUST SENSE YOUR FEELINGS, EXPAND IN THEM. LET THE EMOTION FILL YOU, LET IT BUILD. GET IN TOUCH WITH YOUR FEELINGS.

NOW, WHERE IS THE PHYSICAL CORE OF THE EMOTION? FOCUS.

WHERE DO YOU FEEL THE FEELING? IDENTIFY THE SINGLE CENTER OF THE FEELING THAT STANDS OUT; FEEL YOURSELF INTO THAT CORE; FEEL YOURSELF FLOW INTO THE FEELING.

IN YOUR IMAGINATION, SCAN YOUR BODY.

WHAT DO YOU SENSE? ATTEND. EXPERIENCE IT; BECOME AWARE OF IT; FEEL INTO IT TOTALLY, INTO EVERY FIBER OF YOUR EXISTENCE.

ARE YOUR FEELINGS HOT OR COLD? SMOOTH OR ROUGH? HARD OR SOFT? FULL OR EMPTY?

SENSE EVERY PART OF YOUR BODY; PUT IT ALL TO-GETHER, COMPLETELY; SENSE THE COMPLEX SYMPHONY OF SENSATIONS.

NOW SLOWLY, EASILY, LET YOUR FEELINGS COME DOWN.

GRADUALLY, SLOWLY, WEAKER, WEAKER, LET THE EMO-TION GO THROUGH YOUR BODY, SEEP OUT OF YOU;

RELAX, EASY; LET THE FEELINGS WASH AWAY, DRAIN OUT.

LET THAT FEELING DISAPPEAR; RELAX.

COME BACK NOW.

RELAX. EASY. REMEMBER YOURSELF, RELAX.

YOU'RE NO LONGER FEELING THAT EMOTION.

BACK TO FEELING LIKE YOU ARE NOW.

If you have practiced the earlier basic exercises of awareness consistently, reliving that experience is likely to have been fuller, richer, more varied and complex than the original experience. Your body remembered the experience, and now, with your sharper sensory skills, you are able to sense parts of the original experience that probably escaped you when it first occurred.

NOW SIT BACK. DISTANCE YOURSELF FROM THE EXPERIENCE. LOOK AT IT FROM OUTSIDE, FROM A LONG WAY OFF.

LOOK AT YOURSELF AS IF YOU WERE ANOTHER PERSON. THINK ABOUT WHY YOU FELT AS YOU DID.

WHAT CAUSED YOUR FEELINGS?

GET BEHIND THE OBVIOUS. DON'T BE SATISFIED WITH A CONVENTIONAL ANSWER. THINK.

WHAT ARE THE REASONS UNDERLYING THE REASONS YOU HAVE THOUGHT OF?

WHAT WAS IT IN THE SETTING, IN THE OTHER PEOPLE, IN YOURSELF, THAT TRIGGERED THIS SPECIFIC EMOTIONAL EXPERIENCE.

WAS IT SOMETHING SAID—SOMETHING DONE?

DON'T BE VAGUE. DON'T BE GENERAL.

BE SPECIFIC.

DON'T LET YOURSELF HIDE BEHIND THE CONVENTIONAL
ANSWER.

DIG INTO YOURSELF. ANALYZE. UNDERSTAND. AS YOU DO,
YOU'LL FEEL MORE FREE—OPEN—AND TOGETHER.

~~~~~~~~~~~~~~~~

With this exercise you have taken a major step in en-
hancing your emotional aliveness. *Don't repeat it at once.*
Wait. Allow at least two or three hours or longer to elapse
before doing any other exercise. Simply live and do and
don't think about the experience. You've engaged yourself
in awareness of *your* feelings.

Then, when there is another 10 to 20 minutes free, repeat
this exercise—but use a very different emotion. If you
thought of an angry experience the first time, this time
think of an instance of love or of joy, fear or sadness. For
the first few times, think of strong feelings; it is usually
easier to recapture the flavor of strong emotional experiences. Practice using these intense feelings. But as you continue to exercise, you will discover your capacity to relive
more moderate emotions, and you will learn to sense the
more subtle shadings and nuances of your emotional experiences. And then, after a time, you will discover, without
searching, that you are living more fully and deeply in the
feelings of your life.

Moving Away from the Conventional

In previous sections, we have recognized both the im-
portance and limitations of the conventional: the conventions of language and the conventions of thinking. For
example, we discussed the necessity of linguistic conven-

tions for communication, and how our awareness is limited by these conventions. By implication, then, we were suggesting a point of view that we would now like to make more explicit. That is, we believe that a person who lives fully, has an appetite for life with zest and enhanced awareness, is capable of functioning within the normal conventions of his society. But he also has the capacity to see, to sense, to think and experience in ways that *break* the molds imposed by conventional perception, language, and thought. He can free himself from the debilitating effect of meeting the routine demands of life, and view the world and himself from perspectives that are quite new and exciting. Although that is the purpose of everything in this book, in the following exercises we would like you to confront the conventional directly, in order to awaken your capacity to transcend it.

THINK OF SOME OBJECT YOU USE ALMOST EVERY DAY, PERHAPS SOMETHING THAT YOU HAVE WITH YOU AT THE MOMENT.

DON'T PONDER LONG; CHOOSE THE FIRST THING THAT OCCURS TO YOU. WHAT IS IT?

NOW SIT DOWN AND GET COMFORTABLE. TAKE A PEN OR PENCIL AND A SHEET OF PAPER.

WRITE THE NAME OF THE OBJECT YOU'VE THOUGHT OF AT THE TOP OF THE PAPER.

THINK OF HOW YOU USE IT, HOW IT IS NORMALLY USED.

WHAT DO YOU USE IT FOR?

WRITE IT DOWN.

THEN FORGET ITS NORMAL USE.

LOOSEN UP YOUR IMAGINATION. LET YOUR MIND WANDER
TO OTHER USES FOR THE OBJECT.

LIST ALL THE POSSIBLE WAYS YOU CAN THINK OF IN
WHICH THAT OBJECT MIGHT BE USED.

BE WILD, CRAZY, IMPRACTICAL—UNCONVENTIONAL.

SHAKE YOURSELF FREE.

PLAY WITH YOUR IDEAS.

JUST LET YOUR THOUGHTS WANDER.

IT'S A GAME. HAVE FUN. BE SILLY, CLEVER, BIZARRE.
THERE ARE NO LIMITS, NO RULES—JUST YOU AND YOUR
IMAGINATION.

OPEN UP. DON'T BE RATIONAL.

PLAY WITH YOUR IDEAS AS LONG AS YOU CAN. JUST
IMAGINE—AND PLAY WITH YOUR THOUGHTS.

Did you have trouble getting started? Did you write a
few uses down and then block? Did you fall into a rut of
conventional uses? Don't worry about it, that's what most
people do.

An illustration of this exercise might involve the uses of
a spoon as a book mark, door stop, toilet-paper holder, or
you might think it could be used for just about anything
that you yourself imagine—create.

The secret here is to stay playful. Stay with it. The
*un*conventional uses will come. As you write down the
conventional uses and start freeing your thoughts, then
you'll start seeing some of the unusual ones. Don't get too
serious about this. It's not homework; it's not a job you've
taken home from the office; it's not an assignment. Loosen
up. It's a game. Play with your ideas; juggle them; take

funny leaps; have fun. Take the object, turn it around, upside down, stand it on its side, let it swing—play. Try again, on another sheet of paper.

THINK OF ANOTHER EVERYDAY OBJECT. ANYTHING.

WRITE THE NAME OF THE OBJECT ON THE TOP OF THE PAPER, AND TAKE OFF. PLAY.

HOW MIGHT IT BE USED? SPIN OUT IDEAS—OPEN IT.

MOVE IT. HANG IT. FANTASY—STRETCH YOUR IMAGINATION.

PLAYFUL. FANTASTIC. UNUSUAL. MARVELOUS. WONDERFUL USES.

Did you get further this time? Was it easier? More *unconventional*? Did you capture the playful perspective? Did you get too serious? Too constricted? Too "realistic"? Relax—let your imagination work for you.

Try again—and again—and again—and after a while, you'll discover your imagination, the creative capacities in yourself that you were unaware of. Few of us ever tap even a fraction of our imaginative and creative talents. We are much too busy being practical, mature, serious. But with only a little practice we can learn to transcend our normal, everyday functioning—and we can open the enormous reservoir of creative imagination that is in all of us.

Beyond Conventional Perceptions

This exercise is designed to loosen your habitual ways of perceiving and interpreting visual stimuli. In other words—

seeing. Remember, just as in the preceding exercise, there are no right or wrong answers. There is just you, the range of your imagination, and the growing opening in the flexibility of your responses.

ONCE AGAIN, SIT COMFORTABLY AND BEGIN WITH A PEN OR PENCIL AND A SHEET OF PAPER. RELAX.

NOW TAKE 15 OR 20 SECONDS AND QUICKLY DRAW A SIMPLE DOODLE ON THE PAGE.

DON'T TRY TO MAKE IT LOOK LIKE ANYTHING IN PARTICULAR; JUST MAKE A SIMPLE LINE DRAWING THAT FLOWS FROM YOUR HAND.

FREE FORM—LET IT FLOW. AUTOMATICALLY.

LET YOUR HAND GUIDE THE DRAWING; KEEP YOUR HEAD OUT OF IT.

NOW LOOK AT THE DRAWING.

WHAT IS IT? WHAT COULD IT BE?

LET YOUR IMAGINATION GO. WANDER. RELAX. PLAY.

DON'T BE COMPULSIVE. LET THE THOUGHTS FLOW. STRETCH YOUR PERCEPTUAL FLEXIBILITY. PLAY WITH IT.

TRY DIFFERENT PERSPECTIVES. ANGLES. DON'T PUSH. PLAY. DON'T STRAIN.

TURN THE IMAGE AROUND ON ITS SIDE. HAVE FUN WITH IT.

ARE THINGS ON THE SAME PLANE? DO YOU SEE DIFFERENT FIGURES, BACKGROUND INTERCHANGE?

MOVE. PLAY. JOT DOWN EVERYTHING YOU CAN IMAGINE IT MIGHT BE.

To illustrate this exercise, suppose a person drew five little circles: O O O O O. What might they be? It might be looking down on the heads of five bald bartenders standing at attention. It might be the holes made by a papa mole, a mama mole, and three little moles who were scared by a monkey. Five zero grades. Peepholes? It might be just about anything.

Now try it again yourself. First make the drawing, and then let your imagination flow—just relax and open up. Wander—have fun.

Play with this exercise. Practice. Do it as often as you like. But just as soon as you feel any strain, any pushing, let it go, switch off, stop, and begin something else. As with the other exercises in this section, you may be slow getting started. There may be some blocking, some inhibition. But if you stay playful and relaxed, open, you will stretch the range of your perceptual imagination in easy steps, enlarging the scope of your awareness and the flexibility of your perceptual responses to the world. You'll be able to see things from a new perspective.

Beyond the Word

Breaking the word barriers to expanded awareness is a difficult task. As infants we babble; later we speak our first words, and from then on, we practice, imitate, learn, and rehearse the grammar of our language. Little wonder, then, that moving beyond the over-learned rules of language usage is not accomplished easily or quickly. But it can be done. The results of the opening of this language gate can be a verbal flooding; often accompanied by a remarkable increase in fluency, and a parallel flexibility in awareness.

We have found that two related exercises are particularly helpful in accomplishing this flexibility. The first is what we call No-Sense Speech. It's not exactly nonsense; that is, it's not just a random jumble of words. There is at least a semblance of the order and form of everyday language, but there is no effort to convey sense or meaning. There's no need to be understood.

It is very difficult to utter *no*-sense, without falling into total nonsense. When you "click" into the mode of no-sense expression; there is a temporary suspension of the meaning of words and sentences. There is a reduction of the normal self-checks of logic and communication. And then, when you find yourself able to express *no*-sense, the best way to describe the experience is to say that you experience "language pouring from you freely." Afterward, you feel as if your mind has been massaged, and you are much more open, free, loose, and sensitive to new experience.

For most people, it is easier to do this exercise in writing than in speech. Therefore, we suggest you try it first in writing. Then, later on when you've experienced some flowing and openness, you can try it in vocal form.

BEGIN WITH A WORD, ANY WORD.

CHOOSE A WORD THAT LOOKS RIGHT, SOUNDS RIGHT, FEELS RIGHT—

THAT'S RIGHT FOR YOU.

JUST BEGIN WITH A WORD, AND THEN WITHOUT THINKING, WITH NO EFFORT TO MAKE SENSE, WRITE THE NEXT WORD OR PHRASE THAT OCCURS TO YOU.

AND AGAIN, THE NEXT WORD.

BE FLUID AND FREE;

WRITE THE SPONTANEOUS WORDS AND THOUGHTS.

PUNCTUATE WHEREVER YOU FEEL IT;

STOP THE SENTENCE WHEN IT STOPS.

LET IT FLOW IN THE MELODY OF SPEECH—

FORGET THE CONVENTIONS OF MEANING.

OPEN UP AND LET THE WORDS COME.

~~~~~~~~~~~~~~~

Here is a short example of Joel's no-sense speech:

> "Nowhere near cows are not slippers slide fracture, but fragile cones come when all men are not near. Nile is a leaf and the green and the gray, fun if the words will-o-wisp where they lay."

It's certainly not sense, yet it's not quite nonsense. There's some alliteration, even a kind of rhyme, and there is a structural resemblance to English. The form flows. But it doesn't *mean* anything in the way that normal speech or a written passage conveys messages. It simply is. The purpose is the production, the process, not the product.

Harold's no-sense goes like this:

> "Heavens go slowly tumbling away into the night of gravity brushing aside my focus, softly against the moon bus window become left as going around the rule of the river."

Don't try to imitate these styles. These bits of no-sense simply reflect us at the moment we uttered these words. Find your own movement of expression, your own voice. *Your* no-sense experience. No one can tell you exactly what to do. Just begin, let go—let it come as it comes—write freely, automatically. See where it takes you.

Perhaps at first it will not click. Don't worry. Practice. Maybe standard sentences will come out, phrases often used. All right. No problem. Relax. Just try it again. Keep going. Freely. Focus on the shapes of the words, on the sounds; forget the meaning. Just let the words flow. Allow yourself to open up. Be fluid—have fun.

When you discover your own no-sense mode of expression, you'll be able to switch in and switch out of normal language use with practiced ease. Even after ten or fifteen minutes of no-sense speech, you'll be able to switch into normal usage with hardly a moment's pause.

In the preceding exercise, we relied on your implicit knowledge of the underlying structure of language. We took a step away from normal language usage, retaining some of the formal structure, but trying to escape from conventional meanings.

Now we come to the simplest of verbal exercises—and the most difficult to accomplish. Free association, not the free association of separate words that we have already practiced, but taking those separate words and imposing on them an unconventional structure. As before, we are not after hidden psychic meanings, but rather we are trying to free your use of language itself. By free we mean free of restrictions of form, of content, of meaning.

THINK UP A SEQUENCE OF WORDS. SPONTANEOUSLY.

FREE OF THE RULES OF OUR LANGUAGE.

NOTHING LIKE SENTENCES, DROP THE PHRASES—

WORDS. JUST WORDS.

EACH ONE IN ITSELF INDEPENDENT,

UNRELATED IN YOUR OWN AWARENESS.

~~~~~~~~~~~~~~~

At first, phrases will probably occur to you. Or a simple, obvious chain of associations (e.g., table—chair—lamp—etc.). Stop putting phrases together. Break the chain of obvious associations. Indeed, as you practice this exercise, there will be psychologically meaningful chains of association, but these associations will be meaningful at a level of consciousness far below your normal awareness.

This exercise should be done only after you have repeatedly practiced the 2- to 3-minute warm-up exercises we've called Chaining Your Associations. In those earlier exercises, we provided a formal structure that helps ease a person into the free association process. Now that you have developed some skills in association, we urge you to take away all the formal, structural supports. Go it alone—without apparent meaning, without apparent structure. Freely. Begin with a word—any word—the first word that occurs to you. And then, without thought, without reflection, freely associate word after word after word—ten minutes, fifteen, twenty. String out the words. Let them just flow—dance out of your consciousness.

We will not describe the consequences. It's not easy. But try it again and again. If you feel blocked—something resisting the flow—stop. Do something else and come back to it when you feel comfortable. When you are truly able to accomplish this exercise, any description will be superfluous.

Just Three Words

You're in a playful mood again. *Feel* like having some fun. You're relaxed. Comfortable. *Want* to create . . .

imagine . . . fantasize . . . write songs, poems . . . loosen
up some of those spokes. You'll need some paper and a pen
or pencil. Sit down at a table or desk. Relax.

LET YOUR MIND WANDER FREELY

TO THE FIRST WORD THAT COMES TO AWARENESS.

ELEPHANT? FINE.

ANY WORD; WRITE IT DOWN, AND THEN

LET YOUR THOUGHTS MOVE—

A THIMBLE?

WRITE IT DOWN AND WANDER AGAIN.

TO WATER? FINE. WRITE IT DOWN. AND NOW:

ELEPHANT, THIMBLE, AND WATER.

NOW PUT THEM, ALL THREE, TOGETHER.

THEY'RE THE WORDS OF A STORY YOU'LL WRITE;

JUST LET YOURSELF GO, AND WEAVE THEM.

INTO ANYTHING ANYWHERE ANYPLACE.

LET THE THREE WORDS SING OR DANCE OR TALK,

LET THE THREE WORDS TAKE YOU AND TELL A TALE.

GIVE THEM LIFE AND LOVES, SADNESS, JOY.

NO MATTER WHAT HAPPENS,

LET THE STORY FLOW.

AN ELEPHANT WEARING A THIMBLE IN WATER

WAS SEWING A BIB FOR HIS NEWBORN DAUGHTER.

OR AN ELEPHANT WAS HAVING AN AFFAIR WITH A
THIMBLE,

UNDER WATER, FOR SOME STRANGE REASON.

BUILD THE STORY ON IMAGINATION,

MAKE IT FANTASTIC AS YOU CAN.

AN ADVENTURE? ROMANCE? A MYSTERY?

NO MATTER, JUST LET THE WORDS GO.

When it stops flowing, stop writing. Don't force it. Pick three other words—try again. It's not easy, but with practice your stories will move you toward your opening awareness—you'll experience a new part of the world around you, inside of you. You'll discover your imagination.

The Past and Present in Yourself

Now that you've developed the ability to concentrate intensely on imagery such that you can visualize yourself and objects easily, you're ready for this exercise. Remember: get comfortable, feel free. Relax. Be in a quiet place, sitting or lying down.

CLOSE YOUR EYES—SLOWLY. RELAX.

CONCENTRATE AND IMAGINE A STAGE.

IT'S DARK, VERY DARK, AND THEN SLOWLY A SPOTLIGHT
ILLUMINATES PART OF THE STAGE.

YOU SEE IT. VISUALIZE THE STAGE LIGHTING UP.

THE SETTING IS A ROOM IN YOUR HOUSE, WHEN YOU WERE FIVE YEARS OLD.

CONCENTRATE. THE LIVING ROOM? KITCHEN? DINING ROOM?

SEE IT.

AND NOW, ONE BY ONE, MEMBERS OF YOUR FAMILY COME INTO VIEW.

THEY'RE RIGHT IN FRONT OF YOU. ON STAGE. IN THE ROOM.

AS THEY COME ON, PLACE THEM SOMEWHERE.

YOU'RE THE DIRECTOR; CONCENTRATE. PUT THEM WHERE YOU WANT THEM TO BE.

STANDING, SITTING. WHEREVER YOU'D LIKE THEM TO BE.

PUT THEM NEXT TO WHOMEVER YOU'D LIKE.

THERE'S YOUR FATHER, MOTHER. ANY SISTERS, BROTHERS?

PUT THEM IN POSITION.

HAVE THEM TAKE A POSE.

SET THEM. FOCUS IN.

HAVE THEM HOLD THE POSE.

NOW YOU'RE THERE. YOU'RE FIVE YEARS OLD. PUT YOURSELF IN POSITION. IN A POSE.

WHERE ARE YOU? HOLD IT.

SEE ALL THE MEMBERS OF YOUR FAMILY? GIVE THEM EXPRESSIONS ON THEIR FACES.

LOOK. CONCENTRATE.

WHO IS STANDING OR SITTING WHERE? NEXT TO WHOM?

HOW CLOSE ARE THEY?

WHO IS OPPOSITE WHOM?

WHAT'S THEIR EXPRESSION—FRIENDLY, ANGRY?

SEE THEM—AS THEY WERE WHEN YOU WERE FIVE.

CONCENTRATE. RELAX. SEE YOURSELF IN RELATION TO YOUR FAMILY.

ERASE IT.

NOW MOVE AHEAD IN TIME.

YOU'RE FIFTEEN YEARS OLD. CONCENTRATE.

PICK A ROOM IN YOUR HOUSE.

HAVE THEM COME OUT AGAIN—ONE BY ONE. MOTHER. FATHER. SEE THEM.

YOU'RE THE DIRECTOR. PLACE THEM AND GIVE THEM EXPRESSIONS. HAVE THEM REMAIN STILL.

ANY SISTERS, BROTHERS? PLACE THEM.

NOW, YOU COME IN. YOU'RE FIFTEEN; PUT YOURSELF IN THE ROOM—FOCUS.

CONCENTRATE—IMAGINE. SEE YOURSELF IN THE ROOM.

WHERE ARE YOU? WHO IS CLOSE TO WHOM?

SEE IT. HOLD IT. RELAX.

ERASE IT.

IT'S THE PRESENT.

FOCUS IN ON THE STAGE.

THEY'RE COMING OUT.

IT'S NOW.

PLACE THEM. PLACE YOURSELF. FOCUS IN.

SEE THE ROOM. SEE WHERE EVERYONE IS, AND WHAT
THEIR EXPRESSIONS ARE.

CONCENTRATE.

WHERE ARE THEY STANDING? HOW CLOSE ARE THEY
TO YOU? WHAT'S THE RELATIONSHIP?

HOW HAVE THE PAST RELATIONSHIPS CHANGED? REMEM-
BER HOW IT LOOKED WHEN YOU WERE FIVE, FIFTEEN?

NOW, RELAX—ERASE IT.

~~~~~~~~~~

Finding Yourself in Others

In certain respects, each of us is *self* in relation to others.
Harold is Harold in relation to Joel; Joel is Joel in relation to
Harold. All of us reflect, in part, our relationships with all
the significant others of our lives, and thus we can find
something of ourselves in the perspectives of others. I am
me. You are you. I am here. You are there. My being me
and here is in relation to your being you and there. And
your being you and there is in relation to my being me and
here. Yet, my being me and here is also independent of you
and your being, as is your being you and there independent
of my being.

If this seems at all confusing or complex, think for a
moment of two significant people who are important in
your life—two others who make or have made a difference
to you. Now think of yourself in relation to each of these
people. In some ways, of course, you are *you* regardless of
the relationships; but in other ways, you are *you* in relation
to one of these people in a way that is somewhat different
from the *you* in relation to the other person.

This exercise is designed to capture and experience some

of these differences in you, thus enlarging your awareness of yourself. It requires the capacity to perceive yourself from the perspectives of others, and this is based on the skills developed in some of the earlier exercises, in particular the 2- to 3-minute exercise Shifting Perspectives. After you have practiced and mastered this earlier exercise, let's see if you can try finding yourself in others.

FIND A QUIET PLACE; GET COMFORTABLE. RELAX.

BEGIN BY IMAGINING YOURSELF INTERACTING WITH ONE PERSON WHO IS OR HAS BEEN SIGNIFICANT IN YOUR LIFE.

IMAGINE ONE PARTICULAR TIME OF INTERACTION; MAKE IT CONCRETE, SPECIFIC.

WHAT WAS GOING ON?

WHAT DID THE PLACE LOOK LIKE?

THE OTHER PERSON? YOU?

IMAGINE IT AS IF IT WERE A PLAY.

SET THE SCENE;

NOW PLAY IT—

BUT PLAY IT FROM THE OTHER PERSON'S POINT OF VIEW.

VISUALIZE THE SCENE.

TAKE THE PERSPECTIVE OF THE OTHER; FEEL YOURSELF INTO THE ROLE OF THE OTHER.

INTERACT, BE THE OTHER PERSON.

SEE IT. FEEL IT. IMAGINE SPEAKING, BEHAVING, AND FEELING AS THE OTHER PERSON IN RELATION TO YOU.

SAY WHAT THE OTHER WOULD SAY. DO WHAT THE OTHER

WOULD DO. PLAY OUT THE SCENE IN YOUR IMAGINATION.

NOW STOP. REFLECT.

HOW DID THE OTHER PERSON EXPERIENCE YOU?

REMEMBER: FROM THE PERSPECTIVE OF THE OTHER, SENSE YOURSELF.

WHAT FEELINGS DID YOU ELICIT IN THE OTHER?

HOW ARE YOU PERCEIVED BY THE OTHER?

WHAT DID YOU LOOK LIKE FROM THE OTHER'S POINT OF VIEW?

WHAT DID YOUR BEHAVIOR MEAN TO THE OTHER?

HOW DOES THE OTHER UNDERSTAND YOU?

WHO ARE YOU FROM THE VIEWPOINT OF THE OTHER?

At first, you may experience the exercise as mechanical, awkward, difficult to achieve. You may feel there's a wall up between you and the other. Yet, as you practice, you will discover the kind of empathy called for in this exercise. The wall will melt. This kind of shift in perspective is something you do without thinking in most interactions, though it's rarely with the kind of intensity and total shift you can achieve by explicit concentration and practice. Repeat the exercise from another point of view.

AGAIN SELECT A SIGNIFICANT OTHER, AND ONCE AGAIN IMAGINE YOURSELF INTO THE ROLE OF THE OTHER.

SET THE SCENE; BE PARTICULAR, CONCRETE. VISUALIZE.

INTERACT; IMAGINE; SEE IT AND FOCUS ON THE PER-
SPECTIVE OF THE OTHER IN RELATION TO YOU.

NOW EXPERIENCE YOURSELF FROM THE VIEWPOINT OF
THE OTHER.

THEN SIT BACK; RELAX, REFLECT.

WHO ARE YOU FROM THE POINT OF VIEW OF THE OTHER?

WHAT DID YOU DISCOVER OF YOURSELF?

~~~~~~~~~~~~~~

From time to time repeat this exercise from a number of different points of view. Each time, imagine yourself empathically relating in the role of the other, and each time discover something of yourself in the other. As you practice, you will learn more of yourself, achieve a wider perspective and a deeper self-understanding. Your awareness will be enhanced, your mind expanded, for as you see yourself as others see you, you will deepen your knowledge of who you are. The walls between you and yourself, and you and others will crumble, and you'll have a new experience of awareness.

Progressive Relaxation and Imagery Flow

We shift now to a somewhat different form of experiencing, basing this exercise on the increased body control derived from the 60-second warm-ups, and your enhanced capacity for imagery and awareness.

Begin by finding a chair, not one that is stiff and upright or too soft and cushioned—something in between, in which you can sit comfortably, relaxed, but alert. For the first 60 seconds, follow the 60-second warm-up breathing and breathing again, on page 29.

RELAX. ALERT. FOCUS INWARD. BREATHE EASILY, SLOWLY, RHYTHMICALLY. INHALE; HOLD; EXHALE.

NOW CONCENTRATE ON THE TOES OF BOTH FEET.

FOCUS. STRETCH YOUR TOES; RELAX THEM; EASY; LET THEM REST.

THE TOES OF BOTH FEET; RELAX; COMFORTABLE; LET ALL THE TENSION DRAIN AND FLOW OUT, SLOWLY, GRADUALLY.

NOW SLOWLY MOVE YOUR FOCUS UP TO YOUR CALVES;

RELAX THEM; SOFT; EASY; CALM. RELAX YOUR CALVES.

MOVE YOUR ATTENTION TO YOUR THIGHS; BREATHE EASILY, DEEPLY; RELAX;

LET ALL THE TENSION MOVE DOWN, THROUGH YOUR LEGS, FLOW OUT; YOUR LEGS COMPLETELY RELAXED;

COMFORTABLE; STRONG; BUT QUIET.

GENTLE. RELAX. EASY.

BREATHE IN. HOLD IT. OUT.

MOVE YOUR FOCUSED ATTENTION UP THROUGH YOUR BODY.

TO YOUR WAIST; BREATHE, AND RELAX; FREE OF TENSION; SOFT, BUT FIRM; EASY; RELAX.

MOVE TO YOUR STOMACH. SLOWLY. CONCENTRATE.

FOCUS IN ON YOUR BODY—AT THE SAME TIME BREATHE AGAIN. EASY.

FOCUS ON YOUR CHEST; MOVE YOUR CHEST IN A SMALL CIRCULAR MOTION. SLOWLY.

NOW STOP. RELAX.

FEEL YOUR CHEST MOVE AS YOU BREATHE;

LET IT GO EASILY, EASY;

LET THE AIR IN, EXPAND; HOLD IT, EASY; GRADUALLY, SLOWLY, LET IT OUT;

NOW BREATHE IN; EXPAND; COMFORTABLY; FREE.

MOVE YOUR HEAD SLOWLY FROM SIDE TO SIDE; TO THE LEFT, NOW RIGHT; EASY FORWARD; BACK;

RELAX THE MUSCLES IN THE BACK OF YOUR NECK.

MAKE A CIRCULAR MOTION WITH YOUR HEAD; RELAX YOUR NECK.

SLOWLY REACH OUT WITH YOUR CHIN, TOWARD YOUR LEFT SHOULDER.

COME UP AND AROUND. SLOWLY, PUT YOUR CHIN UP, HEAD BACK.

RELAX, MOVE SLOWLY, MOVE YOUR CHIN TOWARD YOUR RIGHT SHOULDER.

NOW DOWN TOWARD YOUR CHEST.

AGAIN, CONTINUE AROUND.

STOP MOVING; BREATHE EASY; EASY; GRADUAL; SLOWLY.

FOCUS INWARD; CONCENTRATE; ALL THE TENSION IS DRAINED FROM YOUR BODY.

YOU ARE SITTING COMFORTABLY, EASILY, RELAXED;

TOTALLY WITHIN YOURSELF; CALM; QUIET INSIDE; AT EASE; PEACEFUL.

NOW CLOSE YOUR EYES AND IMAGINE A SINGLE FLOWER. A TULIP OR A ROSE?

IN YOUR MIND'S EYE, VISUALIZE THE PETALS; SEE IT—

THE COLOR, THE SHAPE, THE TEXTURE.

TUNE IN ON IT. FOCUS. IMAGINE THE FLOWER.

THE LAYERS OF PETALS, SEE THEM—UNFOLD THE PETALS. PETAL BY PETAL—OPEN THE FLOWER UP. PEEL. PETAL. PETAL—OPENING—EXPANDING.

REST. RELAXED.

NOW EASILY, GENTLY, LET YOUR IMAGERY FLOW.

LET YOUR MIND EXPAND AND TAKE YOU WHERE IT WILL.

FREELY, SLOWLY, LET THE IMAGERY CHANGE;

SEE ONE IMAGE FLOWING INTO ANOTHER, AND THEN IT FADES, GROWS DIM; ANOTHER APPEARS.

LET IT GO.

VISUALIZE. RELAX. FLOW EASY.

SEE THE IMAGES.

BREATHE EASILY, SLOWLY.

COME BACK, SLOWLY. OPEN YOUR EYES. LOOK AROUND.

STRETCH. FURTHER. REACH. STRETCH. FEEL THE MUSCLES IN YOUR FINGERS. STRETCH. RELAX.

The success of this exercise clearly depends upon co-ordination of a variety of skills in awareness that you have previously developed. Your first few times with this exercise, you may have some difficulty achieving the highest degree of coordination possible. Simply practice; with time, it will come easily. The flow of imagery depends upon maintaining complete body relaxation. If, in the course of progressive relaxation, you feel one area of your body becoming tense, stop, focus on that area, concentrate—and relax. Feel relaxed before moving on.

You may have to work up to the full exercise in stages, beginning with progressive relaxation. If you cannot reach total relaxation in 10 or 12 minutes, stop and practice only this first stage of the exercise. Just get the tension out of your body—by concentrating and breathing. Then, after you have mastered this first stage, move to the imagery. If you have trouble achieving a clear and distinct image, don't push it. Stop. Come back to the exercise later. Get comfortable, begin with relaxation, and then try for the image once more. Repeat until you can see, touch, smell the flower and unfold the petals in your imagination, and then let the image recede and let other images flow.

Crossing Sensory Modes

In our first set of 60-second warm-ups, we focused on each mode of sensory experience separately. Thus, you practiced such things as looking and seeing, listening and hearing, touching and feeling—sharpening your sensitivity in each mode of sensation. Now, let's see if you can cross modalities, discover the unity of experience, and thereby enrich your totality of awareness.

From Sound to Sight

For this exercise, you'll need some sheets of paper, crayons, pastels, or colored marking pens—anything you can use to create a visual stimulus, in color. Also, you'll need some music: a recording of any kind of music that you like. It doesn't matter whether it's rock, folk, or classical. Find a comfortable position standing, or sitting at a table, or even on the floor. Put the paper and crayons in front of you. Start the record or tape.

LISTEN—AND HEAR. RELAX.

FOR THE FIRST 60 SECONDS, BREATHE AND BREATHE AGAIN FOR A WARM-UP,

FOCUSING ON THE SOUNDS, LISTENING AND HEARING. RELAX AND ATTEND.

FOCUS AND CONCENTRATE. LOSE YOURSELF IN THE MUSIC.

HEAR IT. GET INTO THE MUSIC.

AND THEN, SLOWLY, BEGIN TO DRAW; LET YOUR ARM LEAD THE WAY.

MOVE IT FREELY. DRAW—NOT AN OBJECT, NOT A FIGURE, NOTHING EXTERNAL:

DRAW THE MUSIC.

UNITE YOUR DRAWING WITH THE SOUND, THE EXPERI-ENCE OF THE SOUND IN YOURSELF.

USE WHATEVER COLORS FEEL RIGHT; LET YOUR BODY AND FEELINGS FORM THE LINES; KEEP YOUR HEAD OUT OF IT;

LET THE MUSIC POUR THROUGH YOU INTO YOUR ARM AND ONTO THE PAPER.

DON'T TRY TO CONTROL IT; DON'T PLAN IT;

LET IT FLOW SPONTANEOUSLY;

LET THE MUSIC LIVE IN YOUR MOVEMENT, IN THE COLORS, IN THE SHAPES, IN THE LINES.

NO WORDS, NO THOUGHTS.

RELAX, LET YOURSELF GO, AUTOMATICALLY,

TRUST YOURSELF, FLOWING,

LET THE MUSIC FILL THE PAPER.

LISTEN AND HEAR—LOOK AND SEE.

~~~~~~~~~~~~

Don't worry about creating great art; don't worry about creating any sort of product. You're not a manufacturer. You're experiencing—engaging in the experience. If you like the picture that develops, fine—but that is incidental. The focus of this exercise must be the experience itself, the feeling of the music flowing through your body and onto the page.

The most frequent difficulty encountered in this exercise comes from the tendency to "make a picture." People begin to plan the design, strive for aesthetic balance, become clever, rational—and of course ruin the experience. Guard against this by focusing on the music; trust your body and feelings to respond. Relax. It doesn't have to look like anything. As a matter of fact, this entire set of exercises might appropriately be called Trusting Yourself, for that is the key to success in this kind of experience. Free your mind. Don't try to figure it out; don't plan an aesthetically pleasing design; withhold critical judgment; simply do, encounter, and experience your own doing.

Of Sight and Sound

Now we can try a slight variation. This time, the aim is to create both visual and auditory patterns simultaneously.

AGAIN, BEGIN WITH PAPER AND ANY DRAWING OR COLORING MATERIALS.

NOW RELAX.

START ANYWHERE ON THE PAPER AND DRAW A CONTINUOUS LINE, HUMMING WHILE YOU DRAW.

FREELY. DON'T PICK UP YOUR ARM. DON'T STOP.

FOCUS ON THE DRAWING. LET THE LINE LEAD YOUR HUM—LOUDER, SOFTER, UP OR DOWN; SWEETER, GROWLING, FAST OR SLOW.

THE HUM CAN BE ANY SOUND OR VOCALIZATION YOU FEEL.

NOW ADD ANOTHER COLOR TO YOUR DRAWING, AND LET THE COLOR CHANGE YOUR VOICE.

JUST SEE AND CONCENTRATE ON THE VISION.

LET THE SOUND OF YOUR VOICE FOLLOW YOUR EYES.

MERGE THE TWO IN YOUR EXPERIENCE, FEEL THE MIXTURE.

SIGHT AND SOUND BECOME ONE DIMENSION OF YOUR BEING.

THEY ARE INTERACTIVE—INTEGRATED. FEEL AND EXPERIENCE THE COMPOSITE.

This exercise, of course, is a simple variation of the more or less common practice of singing or whistling while you work. But with sharpened sensory awareness and the capacity for focused concentration, the experience takes on new meaning. Once again, don't try to be clever. Forget what your voice sounds like. You're not trying to compose anything; the product is unimportant. Attend only to the doing, to the merging of sight and sound—the feeling of the experience.

Feeling Inward and Seeing

GET COMFORTABLE. DRAWING MATERIAL HANDY.

BEGIN WITH THE 60-SECOND WARM-UP CALLED FEEL-ING INWARD.

IF YOU HAVE PRACTICED THIS EXERCISE, YOU SHOULD READILY SENSE YOUR BODY.

NOW FOCUS ON ONE AREA, ONE PART OF YOUR BODY.

EXPERIENCE IT. CONCENTRATE; BEGIN TO DRAW.

RELAX. LET THE FEELING IN YOUR BODY GUIDE THE LINE, THE FORM, THE COLOR;

LET THE FEELING FLOW THROUGH YOUR ARM TO THE PAPER.

DON'T THINK ABOUT IT; NO WORDS. JUST THE FEELING FLOWING ONTO THE PAPER.

DON'T TRY TO BE CONSCIOUSLY "EXPRESSIVE."

WITHOUT THINKING, WITHOUT JUDGING, MERGE AND MIX THE FEELING IN YOUR BODY WITH THE DRAWING.

LET THE SENSE OF YOUR OWN BODY GUIDE YOUR HAND ON THE PAPER—

LET IT BE FLUID. FREE. EXPERIENCE THE MOVEMENT

FROM INWARD TO OUTWARD.

FEEL IT.

~~~~~~~~~~

Thinking the Unthinkable

All of us live with certain beliefs, attitudes, assumptions, expectations and cognitive sets that form the framework of our everyday lives. The creative geniuses, the great poets, artists, scientists, sometimes break this framework, this structure, when they take their creative leaps forward. They change our ways of seeing, thinking, and experiencing the world. They move out, opening a door to experience. For example, in developing the theory of relativity that changed all subsequent views of physics, Einstein defied one of the fundamental assumptions underlying all previous scientific as well as common sense thinking. What if energy and mass were not, in fact, two separate and distinctly different phenomena? This was not all, for his famous equation, $E=MC^2$, posed the equivalence of energy and mass, and changed the history of thinking. Similarly, Picasso asked: What if we could see an object from different perspectives at the same time? And the result was a revolution in modern painting. Yes, new ways of thinking and seeing.

Few of us can be creative geniuses of the status of Einstein or Picasso, but we can profit from their ways of thinking. We needn't concern ourselves with creating a new physics, a new form of painting; but we can and do concern ourselves with creating new awareness—of breaking our old sets—our old framework. So let us borrow an exercise from these creative giants that will help us break out of our own conventions of thought and experience.

We might call this exercise *"what if"* or "making the

impossible possible." There are two stages to it, the first concerned with formulating the *what if's*, thinking of the impossible; and the second, with following up these *what if's* and making them possible.

Stage One: Formulating *what if's*.

This exercise requires a playful mood; it's fun. So if you're feeling too serious, try something else for now. Come back to it some playful time. You'll need pencil and paper to keep track of your *what if's*.

BEGIN TO THINK ABOUT SOME COMMON ASSUMPTIONS, SOME OF OUR UNQUESTIONED BELIEFS AND EXPECTA-TIONS,

SOME OF THE "LAWS" OF OUR THINKING.

AND THEN ASK,

WHAT IF THAT WEREN'T SO? WHAT IF IT WEREN'T SO FOR JUST FIVE MINUTES?

REMEMBER: NOTHING IS SACRED, NOTHING TOO TRUE, TOO OBVIOUS TO ASK WHAT IF.

FORGET ABOUT LIVING REASONABLY; FORGET COMMON SENSE; FORGET BEING RATIONAL.

PLAY WITH YOUR IDEAS; BE BRAVE ENOUGH TO RISK SILLINESS, ABSURDITY, IRRATIONALITY.

REMEMBER: HAVE FUN. BE FREE AND FLUID. THINK OF THE THINGS THAT APPEAR TO BE IMPOSSIBLE.

Just to get you started, here are a few *what if's* we've sometimes played with:

What if you could be in two places at once?

What if time moved backward instead of forward?

What if people walked on their hands instead of their feet?

What if we were all nocturnal animals—stayed up all night and slept all day?

What if everyone were both male and female?

What if you lived forever?

Remember, don't try to be profound, too serious, too realistic. Just relax. Think of anything, look anywhere, and ask *What if?*

Stage Two: Following up your *what if's?*

NOW CHOOSE ANY ONE OF THE WHAT IF'S YOU'VE DREAMED UP;

CHOOSE ONE THAT SEEMS MOST PLAYFUL, MOST FUN TO FOLLOW UP.

RELAX. SIT BACK AND IMAGINE YOUR ANSWER.

MAKE IT POSSIBLE. FEEL IT AS POSSIBLE.

WHAT IF YOU COULD BE IN TWO PLACES AT ONCE? WHICH PLACE WOULD YOU LEAVE IF THE TELEPHONE RANG IN BOTH PLACES?

CAN YOU SEE YOURSELF IN THE "OTHER" PLACE?

WHO WOULD BE WITH YOU?

IN WHICH PLACE?

WHAT IF TIME MOVED BACKWARD INSTEAD OF FORWARD?

WHAT WOULD IT BE LIKE TO BE UNBORN?

EXPERIENCE IT AS POSSIBLE. WOULD YOU CELEBRATE UNBIRTHDAYS? LIVE FOREVER?

WHAT WOULD YOU DO?

PLAY WITH YOUR IDEAS; HAVE FUN WITH THEM. BE LOOSE, ABSURD, OUTRAGEOUS, IRRATIONAL—CREATIVE, DIFFERENT, NOVEL.

SOLVE THE IMPOSSIBLE. NO CONCERN WITH THE PRODUCT; IT DOESN'T MATTER; THAT'S NOT THE POINT.

~~~~~~~~~~~~~

But what is the point? *The Process! The Experience!* Embrace thinking the unthinkable, making the impossible possible, for in the process you will shake some of the cobwebs out of your thinking. You will clear out some of the corners, some of the dust, and what was rust will shine. You will stretch your awareness, discover a new dimension of yourself, expand your mind and consciousness.

Moving Your Body Around and About

You've done all of the basic exercises and dipped into the complex ones. They've opened up your consciousness, your sense of touch, taste, feelings of yourself—the imperceptible has become perceptible. You've come out of the bondage of your old perceptual and cognitive sets. You can concentrate, selectively attend, focus, and imagine. Now we'd like you to try to further expand your awareness by loosening up your entire body and its movement through space.

You need to find a fairly large room, one that's relatively empty of furniture—a place where you can move around freely—without the danger of banging into or breaking anything. A gym would do—or if the weather permits, a place outside. In the country, a large backyard, a quiet place in the park. Ideally, a place that's serene, where you won't be interrupted—grassy, rolling hills, etc.

Be comfortably dressed, wear little in the way of clothing. The clothing you do wear should be loose so that it doesn't interfere with your movements. Take off your shoes and socks.

START BY DOING THE BASIC 60-SECOND BREATHING EXERCISE.

BREATHE IN — HOLD — OUT. SLOWLY — RELAX. DON'T THINK.

START MOVING. MOVE YOUR BODY. RELAX LOOSEN UP.

LET YOUR ARMS HANG LOOSELY. SHAKE THEM. EASILY— LET THEM FLAP. LET THEM GO—DON'T PLAN ANYTHING.

FOCUS ON YOUR BODY. BE LOOSE. COMFORTABLE. YOUR BODY WANTS TO MOVE—MOVE YOUR BODY, LOOSELY.

LET GO—IN ANY WAY. DO WHAT FEELS RIGHT—DON'T THINK ABOUT IT.

YOUR MOVEMENTS MAY FLOW, BE ABRUPT, SLOW, FAST.

IT DOESN'T MATTER—JUST LET THE MOVEMENT COME OUT OF YOUR BODY.

AS ONE PART MOVES, IT WILL BRING ALONG OTHER PARTS—

FOLLOW THE MOVEMENT.

LET THE MOVEMENTS EMERGE FROM ONE ANOTHER— FROM YOU.

GET INTO THE MOVEMENTS.

STEP, RUN, LEAP, TWIST, TURN, FLAP, SHAKE, SWIM, ROLL, SLIDE ALL THE PARTS OF YOUR BODY.

STAY LOOSE.

MOVE EFFORTLESSLY.

BREAK YOUR INHIBITIONS—EXPLORE—

EXPAND YOUR BODY MOVEMENTS.

DO IT FOR HOWEVER LONG YOU WANT.

BE EXPRESSIVE. BE AWARE. FEEL INTO THE MOVEMENT.

FEEL THE AIR PASSING AS YOU MOVE.

FEEL THE PULL OF GRAVITY.

LET IT BE EASY, LIGHT.

MOVE IN TOWARD YOURSELF.

MOVE OUT. STRETCH. EMERGE. FLOW.

STOP WHEN YOUR BODY FEELS LIKE STOPPING. RELAX.

Notice how you feel. Remember the feeling of free body movements. Concentrate and get an image of yourself. How you felt moving. How was it different from all the other body movements you make in the course of a day? Return to this exercise—with practice you'll feel looser and looser—becoming more sensitive to your body movements will expand your consciousness.

Epilogue

~~~~~~~~~~~~~~~~

If you have both practiced and experienced the 60-second warm-ups, the 2- to 3-minute exercises, the 10 to 20 minutes of mind expansion—you have changed your moments of static existence to new levels of awareness and expanded consciousness. You are more aware of yourself. But this is only a commencement, a beginning, for mind expansion is an organically developing process. There is in each of us the capacity for continuous growth, if we only give ourselves the chance. In some small way, the exercises we have described can help you engage yourself in living a fuller, more integrated life.

As you practice the exercises, as you learn and re-learn to experience, new possibilities will emerge, and new ideas for further exercises will occur to you. We urge you to try them out; not all of them will be successful, but you will discover some that are right for you. Practice them, modify them, use them in developing your own unique style of mind expansion, for as you gain new insights you will also discover the most important of discoveries—yourself.

FREEING YOUR ASSOCIATIONS
(listing words as they occur to you)

COLUMN 1	COLUMN 2	COLUMN 3

FREEING YOUR ASSOCIATIONS

COLUMN 1	COLUMN 2	COLUMN 3

SATIATING YOUR ASSOCIATIONS
(writing the same word)

COLUMN 1	COLUMN 2	COLUMN 3

SATIATING YOUR ASSOCIATIONS

COLUMN 1	COLUMN 2	COLUMN 3

About the Authors

Born in New York City, Harold Cook moved to California where he received his Ph.D. from the University of California at Los Angeles in 1967. He has been on the faculty at Syracuse University, a National Institute of Mental Health Postdoctoral Fellow and now Associate Professor of Psychology at Teacher's College, Columbia University. He has presented papers at various national and international professional meetings and been published in several psychological journals. He spends most of his free time trout fishing, and enjoys eating, walking, talking, traveling, loving and living gently.

Joel Davitz grew up in the Midwest, where he was born. He received a Ph.D. in psychology from Columbia University in 1951, and since that time has been a Ford Foundation Fellow, and on the faculty at Yale and Columbia. He has written and edited several books on topics such as emotion, communication, and education, and published numerous articles in psychological journals. A professor of psychology at Teacher's College, Columbia University, he is married (to a psychologist), has two children, and spends much of his free time painting, sculpting and playing tennis.